SPECIAL COMMEMORATIVE BOOK

ORANGE RUSH

Mark Reis, The Gazette

The Gazette
gazette.com

Denver running back C.J. Anderson dives into the end zone to give the Broncos a 24-10 lead against the Carolina Panthers late in the fourth quarter of Super Bowl 50. (Christian Murdock, The Gazette)

Copyright © 2016 The Gazette

No part of this publication may be reproduced, stored in a retrieval system, or transmitted in any form by any means, electronic, mechanical, photocopying, or otherwise, without prior written permission of the publisher, Triumph Books LLC, 814 North Franklin Street; Chicago, Illinois 60610.

This book is available in quantity at special discounts for your group or organization.
For further information, contact:

Triumph Books LLC
814 North Franklin Street
Chicago, Illinois 60610
Phone: (312) 337-0747
www.triumphbooks.com

Printed in U.S.A.

ISBN: 978-1-62937-152-8

The Gazette
Book / Sports Staff
Editor: Matt Wiley
Writers: Brent Briggeman, Paul Klee, David Ramsey
Copy editors: Scott Kaniewski, Jim O'Connell, Joe Paisley, Kate Shefte
Sports designer/graphics: Sean Kristoff-Jones
Editorial assistant: Carlotta Olson
Photographers
The Gazette: Jerilee Bennett, Christian Murdock, Mark Reis, Stacie Scott
Additional photos: The Associated Press
With special thanks to Gazette staff that assisted with planning and distribution: Kevin Miller, Brad Howard, Rich Williams, Chelsey Walker, Mark Bittle, Sabrina Brown, Samuil Nikolov and Dan Steever.

Content packaged by Mojo Media, Inc.
Joe Funk: Editor
Jason Hinman: Creative Director

Front and back cover photos by Christian Murdock, The Gazette.

This is an unofficial publication. This book is in no way affiliated with, licensed by or endorsed by the National Football League or the Denver Broncos.

Mark Reis, The Gazette

CONTENTS

Introduction 6
Super Bowl 50 vs. Carolina 10
Coaching Staff 24
Regular Season 28
Von Miller 40
Brock Osweiler 80
Peyton Manning 104
Divisional Playoff vs. Pittsburgh 110
Defense 116
AFC Championship vs. New England 122

INTRODUCTION

What a rush!

Ever since John Elway signed Peyton Manning to play quarterback for the Denver Broncos the initiative was clear: Win a Super Bowl.

"We don't have a Plan B," Elway proclaimed the day Manning was acquired.

Finally on Feb. 7, 2016, the Broncos reached their goal of capturing a third Super Bowl title by beating the Carolina Panthers 24-10 in Super Bowl 50 in Santa Clara, Calif.

After disappointing playoff losses to the Baltimore Ravens, Seattle Seahawks and Indianapolis Colts the past three seasons, Elway called for change. He said he wanted players who wouldn't be eliminated without a fight. He wanted a team that would go down "kicking and screaming" in the playoffs.

He brought in Gary Kubiak and Wade Phillips and they instantly put their stamp on the Broncos. A successful team that was built to score points was suddenly a monster on defense. The high-flying offense took a back seat to the "No Fly Zone" defense.

The Broncos ranked first in the regular season by allowing an NFL-low 283.1 yards per game, racked up a league-best 52 sacks and teams scored only 18.5 points per game against the Broncos.

In the AFC Championship Game, Von Miller was the best player on the field with 2.0 sacks and an interception. Derek Wolfe and DeMarcus Ware put constant pressure on Tom Brady and the Broncos knocked off the defending champion Patriots.

In the Super Bowl, the defense was at its best and Miller was the MVP. Miller's sack and forced fumble, which led to a touchdown against league MVP Cam Newton, set the tone for the game. The Broncos sacked Newton six times and held him to 18-of-41 passing. The "No Fly Zone" defense ranks among the NFL's all-time best and right up there with the "Orange Crush." The Panthers, who averaged 31.2 points during the regular season, were dominated by the champion Broncos.

Full disclosure: It was a privilege bringing you, *The Gazette* reader, Broncos coverage this season. We tried to report on the team as a fan would want it covered. I grew up a fan of the Broncos. I used to sit in a lucky chair and I'd terrorize my mom if she tried to talk to me when the Broncos were on TV. I still grind my teeth when I think about what could have been if Michael Dean Perry had gotten off the field without a penalty against the Jaguars. The Super Bowl losses hurt. They always will. But the joy this team brings to this region outweighs any of the awful memories.

Our staff understands the impact of the Broncos. Paul Klee went to Denver Christian High School. David Ramsey graduated from Denver South

Peyton Manning throws downfield during the third quarter of Super Bowl 50. Manning threw for 141 yards against the Panthers. (Christian Murdock, The Gazette)

The Denver Broncos' 2015 Championship Season

High School. They grew up in Colorado, and know how important the Broncos are to you. Brent Briggeman grew up in Kansas. He saw the power of the Broncos fans, and Elway magic, from a different perspective based on the rivalry with the Chiefs.

In the end, Elway's vision as a general manager came true. The Broncos kicked and screamed their way to another championship.

Does anyone doubt he will devise another plan to get the Broncos back here again?

Matt Wiley
Sports Editor

Above: Broncos coach Gary Kubiak joined Tom Flores and Mike Ditka as coaches to win a Super Bowl as the head coach of a team he once played for. (Mark Reis, The Gazette) Opposite: Sylvester Williams, left, and DeMarcus Ware celebrate with the Lombardi Trophy after the Broncos won Super Bowl 50. (Christian Murdock, The Gazette)

SUPER BOWL 50
FEBRUARY 7, 2016 • SANTA CLARA, CALIFORNIA
BRONCOS 24, PANTHERS 10

DEFENSE IS UNDENIABLE

Lights-Out Performance from NFL's Top Unit Bolsters Best-Ever Comparisons

By Brent Briggeman

Break out the superlatives, because this Denver Broncos defense just sacked its way into the best-ever conversation.

The defense carried the Broncos past Carolina 24-10 in a star-studded Super Bowl 50. The unit forced four turnovers. It scored a touchdown. It notched seven sacks. It held Cam Newton and the NFL's top-ranked offense to 10 points.

Led by an MVP, 2½-sack performance from Von Miller, the defense even managed to push into the background the ready-made storyline of Peyton Manning quite likely riding into the sunset as a champion.

It was that good. It was as good as any defense on this stage. Ever.

"I've never seen a better one," said John Elway, the architect of this defense. "There's no question that they're in the conversation with how they played today."

The NFL ushered out past Super Bowl MVPs as far back as Joe Namath for its golden anniversary, so maybe that feeling of nostalgia was just in the air. But after the game, the Broncos' defense was talking as much about the 1985 Chicago Bears and 2000 Baltimore Ravens as the Panthers team it just dispatched.

Those defenses are synonymous with greatness. And now this one, directed by coordinator Wade Phillips, is too.

"We dominate," defensive lineman Malik Jackson said. "We're a dominating defense week in and week out. We dominate. That puts us at No. 1."

Added cornerback Chris Harris, "Absolutely we're the best."

The defense had to be historically good, because the offense provided little in the way of support.

Manning and the offense put up just 194 yards. They went 1 for 14 on third downs. The only offensive touchdown came with 3:04 remaining, and came when the defense handed Manning the ball just 4 yards from the end zone.

"Our defense has just been, from the get-go, they've been nothing but awesome," said Manning, who completed 13-of-23 passes for 141 yards and an interception before dodging questions about his future.

Broncos linebacker Von Miller strips the football from Panthers quarterback Cam Newton during the first quarter of Super Bowl 50. Malik Jackson recovered the ball in the end zone for a Broncos' touchdown and a 10-0 lead. (Christian Murdock, The Gazette)

Panthers quarterback Cam Newton is sacked by Von Miller, left, and Derek Wolfe in the fourth quarter. The Broncos sacked the NFL's MVP six times. (Christian Murdock, The Gazette)

Newton, who was named the NFL's MVP less than 24 hours before the game, fumbled twice and threw an interception. His first fumble was recovered by Malik Jackson for a touchdown and put Denver up 10-0 in the first quarter.

Carolina closed to within 10-7 and trailed by just six deep into the fourth quarter, but Newton couldn't manufacture a breakthrough drive against the crush of the Broncos' rush. He finished 18 of 41 with 265 yards and an interception.

"They just played better than us," Newton said. "I don't know what you want me to say. They made more plays than us, and that's what it came down to. We had our opportunities."

After the game, Elway, the team's president and general manager, took the microphone and declared that "this one's for Pat." It was an homage to the same words Bowlen, the team's longtime owner, said about Elway when he quarterbacked the team to a title 18 years earlier.

Bowlen, now ailing with Alzheimer's, wasn't on hand to hear the words. But when Bowlen was still at the helm, he handed the keys to Elway to build this roster. Elway first built the league's best offense, then watched that fall apart in the Super Bowl in 2014.

He then decided the team needed to grow tougher and put his efforts toward building the defense.

He, and Denver, now have a championship to show for it.

"Our defense was just special," coach Gary Kubiak said. "And they have been all year long." ■

Linebacker Corey Nelson poses for a photo with the Vince Lombardi Trophy after Super Bowl 50. (Christian Murdock, The Gazette)

Defensive end Malik Jackson recovers Cam Newton's first-quarter fumble in the end zone to give the Broncos a 10-0 lead. (Christian Murdock, The Gazette)

Linebacker Von Miller grabs Panthers quarterback Cam Newton in the second quarter of Super Bowl 50. Miller was named the MVP of Super Bowl 50, finishing with 2½ sacks, forcing two fumbles and making six tackles. (Mark Reis, The Gazette)

Jordan Norwood takes off on a 61-yard punt return in the second quarter of Super Bowl 50. Norwood's punt return was the longest in Super Bowl history and set up a Brandon McManus field goal to give Denver a 13-7 lead. (Mark Reis, The Gazette)

The Denver Broncos' 2015 Championship Season

VON'S VISION NO LONGER CLOUDED

Super Bowl MVP Thinks of Others

By Brent Briggeman

Von Miller had a surprising message after his MVP performance in Super Bowl 50. The message from the linebacker wasn't to Broncos fans. It wasn't to defensive coordinator Wade Phillips. It wasn't even to anybody in the same jubilant locker room.

It was to Johnny Manziel.

"Johnny Man," Miller said in a message to his fellow former Texas A&M Aggie. "I know it's a rough time. I've been in the same situation. Keep grinding. I'm here for you. Keep grinding."

The message to the troubled quarterback was both out of place and perfectly in place, because Miller wouldn't have found himself dancing to a career night without rebounding from his own troubles. He wasn't about to hide from them on this night.

Miller famously battled his own demons. He was suspended. He seemed headed on a path out of the league. But he righted that path, and now, after sacking Cam Newton 2½ times, forcing two fumbles and making six tackles, the only question about his future is just how big the contract will be this offseason.

"As human beings, we're selfish," Miller reflected. "But when you're doing something for somebody else, that's when the magic happens.

"If I could cut this award I would give to Demarius (Thomas), and (Derek) Wolfe and all the other guys. That's what I would do."

Miller's teammates saw the growth. Malik Jackson was with him through the process. And Sunday, it was Jackson who jumped on the ball for a touchdown when Miller stripped Newton of the ball near his goal line in the first quarter.

"He's definitely grown," Jackson said. "He's one of those guys who's definitely a vocal leader. He's calmed down from the partying and getting in trouble and he's taking care of business. It's about growing up, being a pro and taking care of your business. You have ups and you have downs, but as long as you grow from them that's all that matters."

Cam Newton was the top pick in the 2011 draft. Miller was second. There was no doubt on this night who got the better of the two. Miller surged right past his rival, right to the top of the NFL.

And when he got there, he immediately looked down to find a friend to try to lift up. He would have never thought to do that two years ago, when he watched his first Super Bowl from the sidelines.

That transformation, he realizes, has been the most valuable part of Miller's journey. ∎

Super Bowl 50 MVP Von Miller holds the Vince Lombardi Trophy. (Christian Murdock, The Gazette)

NEW BLOOD ON THE SIDELINE

Elway Gets His Band Back Together for a Broncos Reunion Tour

By David Ramsey • August 30, 2015

New blood.

That's what many franchises seek when chasing a championship.

The Broncos are going with a radical alternative.

Old blood.

Proven blood. (Broncos fans are hoping there's no over-the-hill blood.)

Gary Kubiak arrived in Colorado in January facing a simple, immense task. He has to outperform John Fox. That's all.

Remember, Fox won the AFC West four times in four seasons. He claimed 38 regular-season wins in the past three seasons. He directed the Broncos to seven playoff games, including a Super Bowl. (The Broncos played in five playoff games, total, from 1999-2010.)

All those accomplishments failed to satisfy Broncos godfather John Elway, who pushed Fox out the door.

The Broncos will be chasing NFL supremacy with what amounts to a reunited band. You know what we're talking about: One of those collections of aging rockers who hit the road one last time, hoping to recapture the magic and the money and the success of yesteryear.

Elway has assembled quite a band.

He and Kubiak traveled to five Super Bowls, three times as teammates and twice with Kubiak running the Broncos offense as coordinator. After convincing Kubiak to return to Colorado, Elway summoned Wade Phillips to lead the Broncos defense.

And the final, giant step, Elway convinced Peyton Manning to take his aching 39-year-old body and powerful right arm on a final quest to rule the football world.

For Kubiak, this is a homecoming. He labored as Elway's backup from 1983-91. He served as lead coordinator for an offense that carried the Broncos to consecutive Super Bowl victories.

"Obviously, I'm very familiar," Kubiak said. "I know where to go. I know where everything is in the building and all those good things, but football is football. There is a lot of work to do and there's a lot of work to do to put this team together."

After Fox departed the Broncos, a disappointed Elway said he was weary of the Broncos getting kicked around in their final game of the season. The Fox-led Broncos boasted many strengths, but finishing strong was not one of them. In 2011, the

Broncos head coach Gary Kubiak talks with Peyton Manning during Denver's 19-13 win over the Ravens in the season opener at Sports Authority Field at Mile High. (Mark Reis, The Gazette)

Broncos ended the season by getting trampled in the playoffs by the Patriots. In 2012, the Ravens came from behind to win on a freezing afternoon in Denver. In 2013, the Seahawks annihilated the Broncos in the Super Bowl.

And in Fox's farewell, the Broncos timidly wandered to a home loss to the Colts.

"I think if there is one thing that you would like to have and you want to feel — at least in the last game you want to feel like you go out kicking and screaming," Elway said. "When you're right there and I think two years in a row it didn't feel like we went out kicking and screaming because of the fact the way we played the last game."

At that instant, Elway formulated the slogan for his 2015 reunion band.

He also placed a burden on Kubiak's shoulders. Elway and Kubiak are close friends, but both men realize winning is a requirement for their professional relationship to flourish.

Phillips is, like Kubiak, familiar with Colorado. He coached the Broncos defense from 1989-92 before a two-season reign as head coach. He worked alongside Kubiak with the Houston Texans. Phillips, 68, is a football lifer who began his NFL coaching career in 1976 in the latter days of the Gerald Ford administration.

"Hopefully, we're kicking and screaming," Kubiak said. "I am really excited about our defense."

Manning will play the central role in this reunion band. He's the NFL's ultimate regular-season quarterback, but he owns only one Super Bowl ring.

He wants another. That's why he returned to this venerable, aging band. ■

Legendary Broncos quarterback and current general manager John Elway visits the field after the Broncos' grueling 29-13 loss to the Kansas City Chiefs in November. (Jerilee Bennett, The Gazette)

SEPTEMBER 13, 2015 • DENVER, COLORADO
BRONCOS 19, RAVENS 13

LOVE OR LOATHE IT
Your New Broncos Win Ugly
By Paul Klee

It took a while. It took a solid three quarters before the Mile High crowd, full of faith, caught on to the M.O. of these new Broncos.

"DE-FENSE!" the 76,798 bellowed, over and over, until the defense did what it will do a dozen or more times this season — win the game for the Broncos.

"It might have been the greatest defensive football game I've ever been involved in as a coach," coach Gary Kubiak said after he debuted with a 19-13 win against the Ravens and received the game ball from best buddy John Elway in the locker room.

Don't say I didn't warn you. Star Wars numbers are out. Smashmouth is in.

"I think we can be (the) No. 1 (defense), without a doubt, absolutely," said safety Darian Stewart, the man who replaced Rahim Moore and promptly prevented another Joe Flacco heartbreak by intercepting the quarterback in the end zone.

This was a big-picture ballgame if there ever was one. To figure out what it means that the Broncos beat the Ravens by playing beautifully ugly defense, we are smart to forget the present and stop trying to predict the future.

Both are difficult after Week 1, I know.

But we should look at history, and there's enough juicy history between the Broncos and Ravens that we should be able to figure this out. Here's what I thought after Stewart stopped a last-minute Ravens drive, hearts resumed beating and stomachs returned to their upright position:

The Broncos rarely beat the Ravens like they did Sept. 13 at Sports Authority Field. They have beaten the Ravens 49-27, with seven touchdowns flung from Peyton Manning's right arm; they have beaten the Ravens 45-34, with three touchdowns and 326 yards from John Elway. The Broncos usually beat the Ravens by playing pretty and fun and with gaudy fantasy numbers. But they rarely beat the Ravens by thumping them over and over until the Ravens have no choice but to say "Uncle."

"The way we won today is a big step," Kubiak said.

There was a time Broncos Country feared the Ravens the most. The Raiders were still annoying, the Patriots were becoming the Patriots, but the Ravens were just plain ol' bad news around here. Baltimore won four straight, the Broncos managing more than 13 points only once. The

Broncos wide receiver Demaryius Thomas vaults two Ravens defenders on a 10-yard reception for a first down in the fourth quarter of Denver's win over Baltimore. (Mark Reis, The Gazette)

Broncos would bring their lunch money to the game just for Ray Lewis to take it.

The game was that, only reversed. It seemed Flacco carried a winning lottery in his pocket, and DeMarcus Ware, Von Miller and Brandon Marshall were hellbent on being the lucky ones to cash it in. The Ravens set franchise records last season on offense. In Week 1, they had 38 total yards at halftime. Flacco was sacked twice and threw two picks. The clincher came from Stewart, who last played for — wait for it — the Ravens.

"Physical, hard-nosed football," Stewart said the previous week. "That's why they're successful."

The crippler came from Aqib Talib, a 51-yard interception return for a TD. Mile High erupted like everyone learned they don't have to go to work Monday.

This defense is the best defense Manning has played with. Is he cool with being the opening act? While it's true Manning and Kubiak appear to be reading from different pages of the playbook, the highway to a championship in Super Bowl 50 was never going to be driven with the 39-year-old quarterback at the wheel.

The defense must do the driving. Against the Ravens, it was vroom, vroom, boom, boom.

Oh, it took the Mile High crowd most of the game to grow comfortable rooting for sacks and fumbles more often than 70-yard bombs.

The Broncos tried to win a Super Bowl by dizzying the scoreboard operator until his typing fingers went numb. Now they will try to win one by thumping the opponent until it waves a white flag, and the defense picks it off. ■

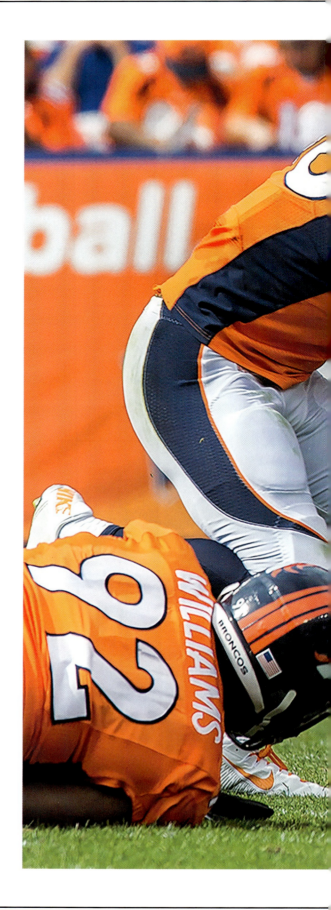

Broncos defenders David Bruton, Jr., left, and Danny Trevathan shut down Ravens running back Javorius Allen. (Christian Murdock, The Gazette)

SEPTEMBER 17, 2015 • KANSAS CITY, MISSOURI

BRONCOS 31, CHIEFS 24

KICKING AND SCREAMING

Broncos Prevail over Chiefs in 31-24 Win

By Paul Klee

They wanted kicking and screaming.

This was Peyton Manning's tomahawk chop.

"What were we down?" linebacker Brandon Marshall asked late Thursday night in the winning, partying locker room at Arrowhead Stadium. "14-0? 21-0?"

Yes, and almost. The Broncos were down, and counted out. But they kicked, screamed, flailed, thumped, clawed, chopped. They won over the Chiefs, 31-24.

Let him be, let him be. Let Manning be.

In his corner, the ol' quarterback showed grass stains on his left thigh, a hint of blood on his right. He sent text messages, maybe to Tom Brady, maybe to others who speculated loudly for everyone to hear his run was done. Chop that up, too.

"He's been taking so much heat the last couple years," wide receiver Demaryius Thomas said from a few feet away. "He just goes out and does his thing."

His thing is making Missouri miserable: 14-1 against the Chiefs, none more improbable, more Chief-y than this one. What happened to Kansas City?

"The turnovers (five) and penalties (nine) killed us," Hall of Fame quarterback Len Dawson said in an elevator.

So did Manning, again. The Broncos trailed 24-17 when Manning sheriff'ed a 10-play, 80-yard drive, capped by a touchdown to Emmanuel Sanders.

Arrowhead Stadium went from red to dread.

Surely the Chiefs would take a knee, force overtime, right? That's what Marshall, Thomas and DeMarcus Ware figured. But Kansas City didn't. Kansas City handed off to Jamaal Charles, a sure thing most nights, but this wasn't most nights.

"I dove and hit the ball out," Marshall said. Bradley Roby, the second-year cornerback, scooped the ball.

"Next thing I see is Roby getting up and running with it," Marshall said.

Nobody wearing red caught him. Two touchdowns in nine seconds. One collective broken heart in a sea of 76,404. One giddy visitors locker room with a 39-year-old quarterback grinning in the corner.

"It just shows the character of this team," Roby said.

The Broncos trailed 14-0, 17-14, 24-17. They looked awful, OK, and, finally, charmed. But they kicked and screamed until Arrowhead became a ghost town.

Broncos cornerback Bradley Roby runs for a touchdown after recovering a fumble by Kansas City Chiefs running back Jamaal Charles during the second half of the Broncos' 31-24 win. (Associated Press)

On "Red Thursday" in Kansas City, the Chiefs shot fire into the sky and banged a drum. They smelled blood, figuratively, and thought this was their chance, literally.

Manning responded: I am old, but I am bold. Let him be, let him be.

Manning was 26 of 45 for 256 yards and three touchdowns and one interception and yada, yada, yada. The way Denver beat the Ravens and Chiefs should be an indication stats are not the thing.

When Manning was pinched into the new offense, he had cable. When he time-traveled back to the high-flying offense, he had DirecTV.

"He's a Hall of Famer," Roby said.

Was Manning perfect? Far from it. Does he have to be? With this defense, far from it. But once the Broncos let him be, to do his thing, he made Missouri miserable, again.

Thomas said he called the Charles fumble, that he stood on the Broncos sideline and told his buddies the Chiefs would drop the ball onto the turf.

"Bubba, didn't I call it?" Thomas shouted across the locker room.

"He called it," Caldwell said.

"DT needs to keep calling it," Ware added from across the way.

Maybe the masses should continue calling out Manning, saying he looks frail, tired and old.

"The game is not done until the clock turns off," Ware said.

Manning's clock is ticking, and hasn't gone off. He's just over in the corner, kicking and screaming. ■

Broncos wide receiver Emmanuel Sanders eludes Chiefs defensive back Jamell Fleming as he scores a touchdown. Sanders had eight catches for 87 yards and two touchdowns on the day. (Associated Press)

SEPTEMBER 27, 2015 • DETROIT, MICHIGAN
BRONCOS 24, LIONS 12

FOURTH QUARTER ATTITUDE

Broncos Raise Nasty Level Another Notch

By Paul Klee

They don't particularly care for your well-being, or whether the yellow laundry scattered across the field is aimed at their feet. If you do score a touchdown on their watch, don't expect the extra point, so often a foregone conclusion, to come easy.

"Points are points, man," Broncos cornerback Aqib Talib said. He blocked a PAT.

What continued to develop Sunday at Ford Field is a defense that should be illegal in some states. The Broncos thumped the Lions in the first, second and third quarters, and when the fourth quarter ("Our quarter," linebacker Danny Trevathan said) finally rolled around, they just decided to take the ball away. Twice. The 24-12 win won't win an Emmy for being pretty. These guys would rather win ugly, anyway.

"We put in a little work tonight," DeMarcus Ware said.

So did the officials, you probably noticed. That's becoming a thing, too. Nine penalties were tossed at the Broncos, including one where Sylvester Williams hit Lions quarterback Matt Stafford, one where Chris Harris Jr. was called for a rare pass interference and one where Von Miller drew another roughing-the-passer flag.

The Broncos are earning a reputation for fielding a defense nobody wants to deal with. If the Broncos score 24 points, chances are they will win. Theirs is a defense that hasn't allowed more than 17 — the Chiefs scored 24, but seven came from the defense on a pick-6 — and the defense seems to ramp up its delight when the score is tight and the quarter says "4."

They are also earning a reputation for the kind of physical play that officials watch closely, eagerly, just to make certain it doesn't cross the line. Have they noticed?

"Oh, yeah. We noticed. We knew coming into this game it was going to be called real close, (that) they were going to be looking for stuff," Trevathan said.

Then again, is that a bad thing? If the officials expect the Broncos to play rough and tumble, the opponent must know the same.

"It's not a bad thing," Trevathan said. "I don't think it's a bad thing. We're aggressive. That's how we play. That's how we win."

It's probably worth noting, as the sample size grows to three games, the best defense in the NFL in 2013 and 2014 was the one belonging to the Seahawks. Guess what? The most-penalized team was also the Seahawks.

"There's tone-setter penalties, and there's little ticky-tack penalties," lineman Malik Jackson said

Broncos running back Ronnie Hillman scores a touchdown during the Broncos 24-12 victory over the Detroit Lions. (Associated Press)

"The tone-setter things, we don't really mind those."

Williams, the nose tackle, said his pop on Stafford made sense when the official explained why he drew a flag.

"I get it," Williams said. "They want to protect the quarterback. I pulled back, but not soon enough. I'll be better next time."

The opposing fans streamed toward the exits with 2:28 left in the fourth quarter, which these days is early for a Broncos game. They wore Matt Stafford jerseys (sans the turf stains of his jersey), Barry Sanders throwbacks, even an Eminem jersey with the number "8." Clever.

And by the time it was over and Stafford was walking gingerly through a tunnel in a spiffy suit jacket, the Lions wanted nothing to do with the Broncos beating on them. In the fourth quarter, when this swagtastic defense seems to find a final gear, the Broncos intercepted Stafford (on a juggling act by David Bruton) and made Stafford fumble (on a tackle by Shaq Barrett).

"In the fourth quarter," Trevathan said, "our attitude kicks in."

It's early, but it seems the football world is taking notice that the nasty level of the Broncos' defense is roughly a 12 on a scale of 1 to 10. Sunday's three turnovers gave them 10, their most through three games in 15 years.

"We have drills we do in practice each and every day," Ware said.

The "Roar Meter" on the Jumbotron inside Ford Field ratcheted up to 116 decibels when Peyton Manning was on the field. The Broncos now are letting Manning be Manning. His play calls: 42 passes against 19 rushes, and the new looks like the old.

When Manning was not the cheetah under attack from a blitzing lion, he had more than enough arm strength to sling one 34 yards to Emmanuel Sanders, 45 to Demaryius Thomas. The issue on offense lies with the offensive line's inability to open lanes for the running backs. And that's an issue that can derail a season.

For now, and especially in the fourth quarter, the Broncos are earning a reputation. Even Thomas, whose idea of taunting is tapping your opposite shoulder as he walks away, got into the act. The subtle, reserved wide receiver earned a taunting penalty.

"Guys are playing without fear," Harris said.

There's nothing nice about playing the Broncos, and they sure seem to like it that way. ■

Demaryius Thomas looks to get past Lions strong safety James Ihedigbo. Thomas had nine catches for 92 yards and a touchdown in the win. (Associated Press)

THE DENVER BRONCOS' 2015 CHAMPIONSHIP SEASON

VON MILLER

Vonnie Football at His Best When Spotlight Is On

By Paul Klee • January 31, 2016

The best player in Super Bowl 50 is African-American, constantly dancing, some people don't like him, and no one is making a big deal out of it.

'Sup, Von.

"Howdy," Miller says often.

The biggest stage in American sports was made for a man who once referred to himself as Vonnie Football. Have you noticed the Broncos' eccentric linebacker relishes the spotlight? Oh, just a little.

The dress shoes studded with gold spikes. The fur-trimmed Elmer Fudd hat. Wrapping up his media obligations last week by taking a quick Snapchat.

"Sunday," he said of his self-imposed social media hiatus. "I'm back on Sunday."

For the Broncos to upset the favored Panthers, Miller must perform like the All-Pro pass-rusher who wrecked Tom Brady and the Patriots in the AFC Championship Game. Two ½ sacks and an interception? That's a start.

"The best defensive performance in Broncos history," Hall of Fame tight end Shannon Sharpe said of the 'D' as a whole on Denver's 104.3 FM The Fan.

Miller Time would give Denver a shot at emptying the tank on Cam Newton and the Carolina juggernaut that carry a 17-1 record into Levi's Stadium next Sunday.

In the 2011 draft, Newton went No. 1, Miller No. 2. They share a history.

How Miller got to this point — the eve of his first Super Bowl week, since he missed Super Bowl XLVIII due to a knee injury — is more complicated.

This is Von 3.0. The first iteration earned Defensive Rookie of the Year and piled up a franchise-record 30 sacks over his first two seasons. Von then was a toned-down version of Von now, challenging strangers to games of Connect Four and spending longer than he needs to signing autographs outside Mile High.

The second Von was a ghost. He faced legal issues like traffic tickets and a missed court date, and he faced stuff that threatened his career. Failed tests put him in the NFL's drug program and earned a suspension. He bulked up, his neck disappeared, and so did the free spirit who was happy to explain the difference between "layers and fryers" at his chicken sanctuary in Texas.

Ravens quarterback Joe Flacco throws under pressure from Broncos outside linebacker Von Miller. Miller was selected for his fourth Pro Bowl in 2015. (Mark Reis, The Gazette)

"I wouldn't call it a full (chicken) farm," said Miller, a poultry science major at Texas A&M.

It's always risky to claim someone is a changed man, on the straight and narrow, since we never truly know what's going down beyond the locker room. We just don't. But the Von you see now is definitely not the Von from two years ago.

Since the first week of training camp when Miller declared, "I love this team," he has been a steady stream of sacks (13.5 overall), shenanigans (gifting to teammates underwear "that increases blood flow to their area") and sack dances (if he drops Newton, who wants to bet he dabs?)

"If I was a quarterback, I'd probably be doing the exact same thing," Miller said.

What changed?

"DeMarcus Ware," he said.

Here, let Von tell it.

"You get to see greatness up close and personal," he said. "The coaches tell you this is what leadership looks like. You've got all these greats that come through here, and they tell you this and they tell you that, but having a real-life example just a couple feet from me… Him being my idol, it was just great.

"I get to come in and see what type of shoes he wears every day, how he laces up his shoes, how he comes to work. How does he handle adversity and all that stuff? I got to see it up close and personal. That helped me be the type of person I am today."

Powerful stuff, right?

Consider John Elway's acquisition of Ware in 2014 a double splash. Both benefited Miller, and not by coincidence. One, the Broncos scored a bookend for Miller's pass rush. Two, Elway landed a mentor for Miller, who soon will sign the most

Von Miller celebrates after Tom Brady threw incomplete in the fourth quarter of Denver's 30-24 overtime win over the Patriots in November in Denver. (Mark Reis, The Gazette)

lucrative contract for a defensive player in league history — if he's not hit with a franchise tag.

I asked DeMarcus: How is Von different now from when you arrived in Colorado?

"Von was going through some things off the field, but you have to understand that sometimes you're young for a while and you have to grow up," Ware said.

Simple enough.

Media are trying their damnedest to complicate and turn Super Bowl 50 into a contrived political statement. Labeling quarterbacks by their race makes for juicy clickbait, but don't fall for it.

See, the coolest thing about the games we play is that they don't care. They don't care about your ethnicity, your background. They care about whether you can play. Sports are mostly silly, but sports remain an unbiased meritocracy. In a locker room, race is seldom an issue until outsiders inject it into the situation. Newton being a black quarterback wasn't a thing until media made it a thing. I have yet to meet a person in Colorado who cares about Newton's skin color, only those who wonder this: Can the Broncos beat the Panthers and their absurdly gifted, 26-year-old quarterback?

Without knowing it, Miller offered the freshest take on the black vs. white nontroversy that serves as low-hanging fruit in an otherwise riveting Super Bowl.

"That's one of my favorite quarterbacks," Miller said. "Peyton (Manning) is obviously my favorite quarterback, but other than that, it's Cam."

Real recognizes real, not skin color.

Von 3.0? The best player in Super Bowl 50 recognizes an opportunity. ■

Raiders quarterback Derek Carr fumbles as he's sacked by Broncos linebacker Von Miller in the first quarter of Denver's 15-12 loss to the Raiders. (Mark Reis, The Gazette)

OCTOBER 4, 2015 • DENVER, COLORADO
BRONCOS 23, VIKINGS 20

'MIND CONTROL'
One Explanation for 4-0 Start
By Paul Klee

Do the Broncos have a few screws loose? Or does their unusual explanation for a 4-0 start mean they are on to something Super?

Denver's brand of football isn't perfect. With a running game as moody as a teething toddler and an offensive line bound together with Band-Aids, the first quarter of a long season has been far from ideal — except in the standings.

How do they explain it? "Mind control," defensive end Antonio Smith said as he slipped on a cowboy hat after the latest nail-biter, a 23-20 win against Minnesota.

Come again?

"I guarantee you when that ball is supposed to drop, that team you're going against is wishing they can win," Smith said. "But for some reason we got a mental (thing) that says, 'There's no way I'm going to lose.'"

Smith said he borrowed the explanation from good buddy Von Miller, who addressed the locker room after one of the four times they snatched victory from the jaws of defeat.

"He said, 'They think they're going to win. But we've got mind control over them!'" Smith recounted. "I can't help but laugh every time he says it."

There's nothing funny about the way the Broncos' defense hunts down quarterbacks. Minnesota's Teddy Bridgewater should be proud of the way he got back up after seven sacks — the most by a Denver defense in 19 years — to give the Vikings a chance to win at Sports Authority Field. But when palms get sweaty and the fourth quarter clicks into the final minutes, the Broncos' defense waits for the perfect moment to strike. This time it was T.J. Ward smacking Bridgewater, again, and forcing him to fumble.

The first time it was Darian Stewart intercepting Joe Flacco on the doorstep of the end zone against Baltimore. The second time it was Bradley Roby scooping and scoring at Kansas City. The third time it was David Bruton picking off Matthew Stafford in the Lions' den. With five minutes left in each of the four games, the score has been tied or tighter than six points.

In all four, the Broncos summoned their voodoo and won. Depending on how you view a beer mug — half empty or half full — the Broncos are either walking a tight rope without a net or riding a magic wave. But there's no doubt their confidence soars when it's winning time.

"We knew the play was going to come," Miller

Broncos defensive end Malik Jackson celebrates after sacking Vikings quarterback Teddy Bridgewater during the fourth quarter of a 23-20 victory for the Broncos. (Christian Murdock, The Gazette)

The Denver Broncos' 2015 Championship Season

said of Ward's sack-fumble. "We just didn't know when."

True, the Broncos twice allowed the Vikings to creep into a game that had the look of a blowout. But there's something to Miller's theory, a bizarre as it sounds.

It's a team-wide belief that no matter what happens over three quarters, someone will make a play in the fourth that turns the game in their favor. It's a confidence thing, a swag thing and, for 16 seasons around here, it was a John Elway thing.

"I'm a firm believer that faith moves mountains," Smith said.

With an adequate sample size that suggests 42-14 blowouts are history and 23-20 nail-biters are here to stay, the Broncos have a script and they are sticking to it: Keep it close, keep it close, keep it close. Then, boom!

"Another great day out here at the stadium," Miller said.

The pessimist says that's a precarious way to win a Super Bowl, that Peyton Manning can't have more interceptions (two) than touchdowns (one) if the Broncos are to escape the likes of the Patriots and Bengals, that Adrian Peterson's 48-yard scoring run was a great player making a great play, a precursor to what Tom Brady and Aaron Rodgers will do in November.

Meantime, the Broncos are convinced it's mind over matter, that their fourth-quarter mojo is sustainable all the way through the playoffs.

"There's nothing magic about what we're doing," Miller said.

Seven players were responsible for the seven sacks, a testament to Wade Phillips' varied schemes and the absurd talent that lines the defensive roster.

"Seven, and I only got one," Miller joked.

While the Broncos weren't comfortable with upchucking a 10-point lead, they were 100-percent sure someone would make the big play that sent the thousands of Minnesota transplants in attendance home without a smile.

Yes, the Broncos might have a few screws loose. They also might be on to something. ■

Broncos wide receiver Emmanuel Sanders salutes the fans as he leaves the field after the Broncos' win over the Vikings. Sanders tallied 68 yards on three catches. (Christian Murdock, The Gazette)

OCTOBER 11, 2015 • OAKLAND, CALIFORNIA
BRONCOS 16, RAIDERS 10

WIN DELIVERED BY THE DEFENSE

Defense Waits for Offense to Join Dominating Fun

By David Ramsey

DeMarcus Ware was watching television in a small room in an old, tattered stadium in this city by the bay.

He wanted to rampage beside his teammates, but back spasms sent him to the Broncos training room at O.Co Coliseum. For this entire Broncos season, one defined by an astoundingly talented and violent defense, Ware and Von Miller have competed in short sprints.

The finish line?

The quarterback.

Miller raced alone in the early minutes of the third quarter. He exploded into the Raiders backfield and set his sights on QB Derek Carr.

What happened next surprised Carr. It did not surprise Ware.

Miller ripped the ball out of Carr's hands as the quarterback tumbled to the ground. Miller ended the show by sprinting, football in hand, to the Denver sideline, where the Broncos indulged in a short party amid a sea of stunned fans wearing black and silver.

While his teammates partied, Ware resisted the temptation to start a jump-up-and-down celebration. He rejoiced, but made sure to protect his aching back. (Ware said his back felt "fine" as he walked out of the locker room after the game.)

"Those are plays that great players make," Ware said. "Von is one of those guys. He's not only thinking, 'I need to go in there and get a sack.' He's thinking 'What I can do to win this game?'"

Ware talked in a quiet voice in the Broncos' loud locker room. The Raiders had once again been vanquished, this time 16-10.

"It was an awesome thing," Ware said of the strip sack, "but that's the type player Von is."

It's not only Miller who is inspiring use of the word awesome. It's an entire defense. For the past three seasons, the Broncos were defined by Peyton Manning's right arm. He rescued the Broncos from peril, week after week.

Now, the defense performs the rescues, week after week.

Manning tossed two interceptions and failed to direct the Broncos to a touchdown, although he can't be blamed for the score that slipped through the hands of Demaryius Thomas.

The Broncos' rushing attack was close to invisible. C.J. Anderson and Ronnie Hillman combined for 43 yards on 18 carries while spending the afternoon in the arms of angry Raiders defenders.

Anderson rushed for 366 yards in consecutive games last season. He's stumbled to a mere 139 yards

Broncos tight end Virgil Green is upended by Raiders cornerback Charles Woodson during the Broncos' 16-10 win. The win boosted Denver's record to 5-0 on the season. (Associated Press)

in five discouraging games this season.

He's stubbornly optimistic about Denver's attack.

"Why wouldn't I be?" he said.

Well, maybe because the Broncos' offense scored nine points and required yet another rescue by the defense.

If this defense-first script sounds familiar, that means you're probably getting a little old. In 1977, a mighty Broncos defense carried a not-so-mighty Broncos offense to the Super Bowl. You might have heard of this defense. It was called The Orange Crush.

Midway through the fourth quarter, it was cornerback Chris Harris' turn to save the Broncos. The Raiders trailed by two points, 9-7, and the Broncos' perfect record remained in peril.

That all changed when Harris jumped in front of a Carr pass and set his eyes on the end zone.

"Ah," he said to himself, "they ain't catching me today."

He was right. He raced 74 yards to a touchdown.

After the game, Harris took care to be diplomatic. He's a believer in the wonders of the Broncos' defense, but said he expects his offensive brethren to soon join the fun.

"They're going to start clicking man," he said, sounding like a man trying to convince himself. "We just have to have faith in them, that they're going to get it right."

Faith, as you know, is the evidence of things not yet seen. Virtually every Colorado resident is waiting for Manning and the Broncos' offense to deliver points instead of promises.

But a win delivered by the defense is just as sweet as a 51-48 victory. Here's the moment that will stick with me from Sunday's battle in an old, tattered stadium.

Harris was running off the field as the game ended, and he was met by Billy Thompson, the masterful safety from the 1977 defense. The men are friends who talk often about The Orange Crush of yesteryear and the Orange Crush of right now.

Thompson shouted his approval for the long journey Harris took to the end zone.

"I had to do it," Harris shouted to Thompson. "I had to do it for you, baby." ■

Peyton Manning gestures at the line of scrimmage during the first half of the win over Oakland. Manning threw for 266 yards and two interceptions on the day. (Associated Press)

OCTOBER 18, 2015 • CLEVELAND, OHIO
BRONCOS 26, BROWNS 23, OT

OVERTIME ANGST
Undefeated Broncos Know This Luck Can't Last
By Paul Klee

This isn't going to end well, and I don't mean October.

October will end with the Broncos riding high in the NFL standings at 6-0 and low in the reality standings at "Uh-Oh." It will end with tricks, mostly by the Denver defense and its fourth-quarter voodoo magic, and treats, the looming arrival of Aaron Rodgers and the unbeaten Packers on Nov. 1 at Sports Authority Field.

But this won't end well, and I mean the whole thing, if Gary Kubiak, Peyton Manning and the Broncos' offense continue down this bumpy road.

The Broncos beat the Browns, 26-23 in overtime, and there was angst. Twenty-seven straight drives without an offensive touchdown? What once was a Ferrari is now a Zamboni on grass.

"We are still going through a transition," Manning said afterward, and going through a transition certainly is made easier when you're undefeated, with a bye week to close out October.

The split scene inside the postgame locker room offered a perfect summation of these Broncos. The defense raged into the night, chanting "Shaq! Shaq! Shaq!" in honor of Colorado State's Shaq Barrett, whose 1.5 sacks offered a fine impersonation of DeMarcus Ware. Meanwhile, on the other side of the room, the offense knew the questions, and the schedule, that are coming, and sounded like they'd been sentenced to a full winter in Ohio.

"We're just not finishing," Demaryius Thomas said.

"We're certainly not playing as well as we would like," Manning said. "But we're playing well enough to win."

Here's the thing, though: The Broncos don't need the 2013 Ferrari that zipped past every scoring record in the book. The defense is so dominant, they just need an offense that doesn't mess it up. When the Broncos opened a 10-0 lead and here-we-go-again swept over the 67,431 sardined into FirstEnergy Stadium, it crossed my mind the only way Cleveland could make this a game is if Denver gave it back.

It did. Three times. Manning has 10 interceptions, a number he didn't reach until Week 14 in 2014, Week 15 in 2013 and Week 14 in 2012.

"We're struggling," Manning said.

There's a detachment between the Manning philosophy and the Kubiak philosophy.

"It has by no means been easy, but coach Kubiak and I continue to talk and we are committed to

Broncos strong safety David Bruton celebrates an interception during the Broncos' 26-23 overtime win against the Cleveland Browns. It was one of two interceptions on the year for Bruton. (Associated Press)

trying to get on the same page and get where he and I have a good feel for each other," Manning said. "We are both committed to the cause."

No fault in that. How the Broncos are 6-0 with five wins decided by a single score is something of a football miracle, and in terms of entertainment value these Broncos get two thumbs-up. In the fourth quarter and overtime, there was an Emmanuel Sanders overturned catch; a Browns interception; another Browns interception; the Broncos defense shoving the Browns backward and out of field-goal range after the interception; the muffed punt by Jordan Norwood near the goal line; a 35-yard game-winning field goal by Brandon McManus. Miss anything?

"In warmups the ball was moving from one upright to the other," McManus said of the swirling winds. "It was kind of unbelievable."

Sure has been. How's your blood pressure?

"I won't be going to Vegas for my bye week," Manning said. "I'm not feeling real lucky."

Considering the hectic finish week after week, allow me to suggest a beach hut in Cabo or a bed and breakfast in Basalt. Take the week, channel Aaron Rodgers and R-E-L-A-X.

And pour one out for the poor Browns. Visit Cleveland, and you see why they shed tears and burned LeBron James' jersey. This is St. Louis with a lake, a very cold lake, and their beloved sports teams are what they have and what hold their hearts. Peyton Manning is 7-0 against the Browns.

"This will be my last game in Cleveland," Manning said, assuring the locals.

Can the Broncos host a parade with this formula? Well, Russell Wilson threw four interceptions last season in the NFC Championship Game, and the Seahawks rode a relentless defense to victory, so it's possible. But history suggests this will not end well, even if October did, unless the Broncos offense finds its way. ■

Running back Ronnie Hillman runs the ball during the second half, with Browns defensive tackle Xavier Cooper trailing. Hillman had a big day on the ground with 20 carries for 111 yards. (Associated Press)

NOVEMBER 1, 2015 • DENVER, COLORADO
BRONCOS 29, PACKERS 10

NOT AN UNDERDOG
On Special Night Special Potential
By Paul Klee

This was a rout, never a contest. This was a sandlot game when First Captain gets to make the first seven picks. This was a collection of NFL All-Stars noticing they were an underdog, playing at home, and wondering, You serious, bro?

"Underdog? That pissed us off. I'm not going to lie," cornerback Chris Harris Jr. said.

Oh, the Broncos embarrassing Aaron Rodgers and the Packers, 29-10, was a whole lot of things, but as it pertains to the season ahead, the Week 8 game at Sports Authority Field was this: The birth of a juggernaut. You have a better chance of accurately predicting Colorado's fickle weather than predicting the NFL. But mark down the first day of November as the moment the Broncos sent up a bat signal to show what happens when a team combines a defense out for blood with a Peyton Manning-led offense that looks more like its old self.

Sure it's possible the Broncos fizzle out against the difficult road ahead, and in January. But if they play like that? Good luck.

"We wanted to come out and show the world we're not a team that's going to fade away," linebacker Brandon Marshall said.

It added another layer of swag when the Broncos heard throughout the bye week their 6-0 start was something of a fluke, that they were walking a thin rope.

"I like the monkey on our back. It puts us in the mode we're in now," Von Miller said. "The monkey is good. The monkey is good."

The older guys saw it, too. On a night the franchise honored the first Super Bowl champions in club history, the 1997 Broncos, most of the former players convened in the postgame locker room for handshakes and manhugs with the young bucks. Shannon Sharpe, never at a loss for words, stood in front of the cameras and said just loud enough for Demaryius Thomas to hear: "Don't let DT in my shot."

It takes a lot to impress a Super Bowl champion — not to mention a group that hosted two consecutive parades down Broadway — but the '97 crew marveled at the destruction these Broncos leveled on the previously undefeated Packers.

Rodgers? Seventy-seven passing yards. Total.

"I ain't never seen anything like that," Ring of Fame wide receiver Rod Smith said. "Not with that guy."

The Packers' defense, tops in fewest points

Packers cornerback Damarious Randall tackles Broncos receiver Andre Caldwell after Caldwell's reception for a first down. The Broncos stayed perfect in a battle of undefeated teams with a dominant 29-10 win. (Christian Murdock, The Gazette)

allowed in the NFL? Shown the door by Peyton Manning's 340 passing yards and C.J. Anderson's 101 rushing yards.

"Any time you put your owner in the Ring of Fame, you have to win the game," said Manning, who can break Brett Favre's career wins record next Sunday, fittingly, in Indianapolis. "I think that's kind of a rule."

This was the Broncos taking note of the skepticism about their perfectly imperfect start and the fact they were made a three-point underdog at Mile High.

"Thank you, Vegas," Harris said.

There was a point in the third quarter when the Broncos had committed nine penalties, the Packers had committed one, and the Broncos still led by two touchdowns. There was another point, the end of the third quarter, when the Broncos had piled up 410 total yards and the Packers had 110.

"We were clicking on all cylinders," safety T.J. Ward said.

It was only one game, on "Sunday Night Football," in front of 77,043, including a few thousand Packers devotees who drove in from Highlands Ranch for the big game. The Pats, Bengals and Steelers are still in front of the Broncos on the schedule.

But this was something else. This was sending one of football's great quarterbacks and a 6-0 team to bed without its supper and telling them to like it. ■

Broncos running back C.J. Anderson runs 28 yards for a Denver touchdown against the Packers. Anderson had a terrific outing with 101 rushing yards and a touchdown. (Christian Murdock, The Gazette)

NOVEMBER 8, 2015 • INDIANAPOLIS, INDIANA
COLTS 27, BRONCOS 24

RED FLAG
In Loss, Broncos Learn Lesson the Hard Way
By Paul Klee

You can kick and scream, but you can't poke.

"It wasn't intentional," justified Aqib Talib, a stooge on Sunday.

The eyes have it. That undefeated, idyllic record? The Broncos don't.

Blink, and it was gone, 27-24, thanks to the Indianapolis Spoil Sports. They do three things well here in the Circle City: Race cars in a, well, circle; host big sporting events; beat the Broncos. Denver hasn't won in Indy since 2003 — six straight losses, from the RCA Dome to Lucas Oil Stadium — and saw 7-0 tumble to 7-1.

"Bad day at the office," Talib said.

He was the bad guy, is a bad guy, but isn't the reason for the bad day. Where, exactly, did the Broncos outperform the Colts? On impolite suggestions for Lasik surgery?

It wasn't Talib's eye poke that ruined Peyton Manning's (second) return to Indy, either. The Broncos butchered this one long before Colts tight end Dwayne Allen got an eyeful. But that incident summed up Denver's bad day.

The things that had been working all the sudden didn't work. Frustration ensued.

This was coming, sooner or later. That Packers win wasn't a fluke, but neither were nail-biters against the Ravens, Chiefs, Raiders, Vikings and Browns. Any one of those games coulda been, shoulda been, the Broncos' first loss. But those teams have no Luck.

"I think the blessing and the curse of professional sports is you're on to the next week no matter what happens, right?" Andrew Luck said. He's 3-1 against Manning, and the Broncos would rather not play him again. (The TV networks hope they play again.) But don't be surprised if they do. The Colts will win the crummy AFC South and earn a home playoff game. Then it's off to Cincinnati, New England or, yes, Denver.

Dun, dun, dun.

Luck had zero interceptions, a first for a quarterback against this Broncos defense. He had a quarterback rating of 98.4, also a season best against Denver. Luck and new offensive coordinator Rod Chudzinski stole Manning's show. They made it so very few of Luck's passes were intercept-able, if that's a word. On their best plays, Luck waited, waited and waited, knowing he was about to take a wallop. Then, once half the Broncos' defense was all up in his grill, he calmly let loose a short pass over their heads. Screen passes have a certain sting to them.

The Broncos' greatest attribute has been the

Indianapolis Colts' running back Ahmad Bradshaw hurdles a Broncos defender for an eight-yard touchdown reception. The Colts stymied the Broncos, 27-24. (Associated Press)

aggression of their defense. The Colts used it against them. Then the Broncos used it against themselves.

Trailing 27-24, the Broncos still had a shot, and wouldn't it have been a sweet story if Manning broke the career yardage record (he needs only 3 more) and the career wins record (one more!) on a last-minute drive in his old town?

Eye, caramba. The Colts would've faced a third-and-7 when Allen's eyeball popped out and landed on Talib's finger.

OK, not really. In his defense, let Talib tell it: "I seen him head butt Von (Miller) a little bit, and I went over there to poke his head. My hand slipped a little bit, hit his face. He acted like he got in an 18-passenger car wreck. That's just the type of guy he is."

I can't speak to what type of guy Allen is. But I know — and you should, too — Talib's rap sheet includes arrests for simple battery and aggravated assault, neither of which has anything to do with football, everything to do with a hot temper.

His unnecessary roughness penalty gave Indy a first down. Five snaps later, Talib earned an unsportsmanlike conduct penalty. Why? "Clapping," he said.

"Guess there's something in the rulebook — 'Too hard of a clap' flag," Talib said. "That's the one I got."

It's fun, this above-the-law bravado, until it's January and a Super Bowl bid is on the line. Think the Patriots, who employed him, will attempt to get under his skin?

"You guys ever played football?" Talib asked media in the locker room.

T.J. Ward chimed in: "Nope."

Talib: "You ever lost at the end of the game?"

Ward: "Nope."

Talib: "You remember back to how that feels? That's how I felt. I was just mad."

Anyone who has competed beyond a whiffle ball diamond knows the feeling of what it's like to lose to a team you really don't like. I feel you, man. Losing stinks like bad plumbing.

"We've got to nip that in the bud so we at least have a chance to go win the game," defensive lineman Antonio Smith said of the dumb penalties.

But there must be a limit to the aggression. What makes these Broncos good is also what can make them come undone. It's an all-out attack — at least on defense — that leaves them vulnerable to scrambling quarterbacks and the big play. It also makes them targets to NFL officials, who are on to them.

"It was touchy out there, real touchy," Smith said. "But only one way."

No one in white had a good day. Gary Kubiak failed to toss a red challenge flag when Luck was clearly short of a first down. The Broncos' offense didn't score a point until the third quarter. The defense allowed scoring drives of 80, 63, 63 and 80 yards. Now the NFL has three unbeatens, none in Colorado.

Manning, ever the capitalist, saved his next records for a home game at Mile High. Makes sense. Ticket prices will soar. And he needs only 3 yards to break Brett Favre's mark for passing yards. The wins record seems inevitable. It's the Chiefs, after all.

"We got beat by a better team today," Manning said.

Talib's shenanigans didn't get the Broncos beat. They trailed 17-0 before eye pokes became a thing. But the lasting lesson from Sunday we learned back in kindergarten: An eye for an eye rarely works in your favor. ■

Emmanuel Sanders can't quite make the catch during the first half of the Broncos' loss to the Colts. Sanders had six catches for 90 yards and a touchdown in Denver's first loss of the season. (Associated Press)

THE DENVER BRONCOS' 2015 CHAMPIONSHIP SEASON

NOVEMBER 15, 2015 • DENVER, COLORADO
CHIEFS 29, BRONCOS 13

WARPED RECORD
Staggering Broncos Must Run Their Way to Revival
By David Ramsey

The Broncos' best hope to rescue a suddenly faltering season was sitting in a silent locker room.

After many games, a crowd of reporters gather around C.J. Anderson's locker and TV lights shine on his face. Friendly questions are met with friendly answers.

This was not one of those times. Anderson was alone.

This makes sense. He had rushed twice for 9 yards in the Broncos' 29-13 defeat to the Chiefs that throws an entire season into question.

"I just run what they call," Anderson said to the only person who bothered to talk with him. "I try to do my job to the best of my ability."

Peyton Manning is not the man to rescue these Broncos, who are blessed with one of the best defenses in franchise history and burdened with one of the most unpredictable offenses in football history. Manning is burdened by old age and a damaged body. He will never again be the Manning of 2006, or even 2014.

Brock Osweiler is not the man, either. He might become the quarterback who can carry a franchise, but those days are in the future. Maybe 2016 or 2017 will be Osweiler's season to dominate. It won't be 2015.

A powerful running game, led by Anderson and his sidekick Ronnie Hillman, offers the only way for the Broncos to make noise in the playoffs.

The potential is there, even if the Broncos struggled to only 69 yards rushing against the Chiefs. Last season, when Anderson was healthy, he danced and powered his way to huge games against the Bills and the Dolphins. Manning was struggling with injury, but the Broncos scored 68 points in the wins.

Anderson didn't want to talk about the potential of the running game.

"I'm not going to speak on that," he said in a polite voice. "I feel like that's a question you're trying to put me in to make a controversy. I'm not going to speak on that."

I told him "potential" is almost always a positive word, one that indicates better days could be ahead. I told him I wasn't skeptical.

"You are skeptical," Anderson said, ending our conversation. Well, maybe a little.

Numbers fail to support my strategy for the Broncos, who ranked 28th in NFL rushing heading into Sunday's game. But the low numbers have much to do with emphasis.

This offense was designed to be led by a healthy, prolific Manning and that version of Manning has

Peyton Manning throws under pressure from Kansas City defenders in the second quarter of the Broncos' 29-13 loss to the Chiefs. The loss was the second in a row for Denver. (Mark Reis, The Gazette)

departed our lives.

Over the next few weeks, while Manning mends from rib and ankle injuries and Osweiler matures, the Broncos should slow down the pace, lean on the run and rely on a ferocious defense to keep them afloat.

They also might talk with T.J. Ward about turning down the ferocious meter. He was ejected, with good reason, after punching Chiefs receiver Jeremy Maclin in the fourth quarter.

Ward, like Aqib Talib, doesn't do repentance.

"They were doing cheap things all game," Ward said. "He tried to cheap shot me again … and I got kind of hot."

Notice, there was no mention of regret.

Two weeks ago, the Broncos were soaring after stampeding the allegedly mighty Packers.

Today, the same team is staggering, along with its fans.

The real Broncos reside somewhere between soaring and staggering. This remains a team that can win a playoff game and maybe even arrive in the AFC title contest.

But the Broncos are going to have to run there. ■

Above: Sisters Savannah Roth, left, and Grace Roth show their disappointment in the fourth quarter of Denver's loss. (Mark Reis, The Gazette) Opposite: Quarterback Brock Osweiler looks down field to pass in the fourth quarter during the Broncos first scoring drive of the game. Osweiler replaced a banged up Peyton Manning and threw for 146 yards and a touchdown in defeat. (Jerilee Bennett, The Gazette)

NOVEMBER 22, 2015 • CHICAGO, ILLINOIS
BRONCOS 17, BEARS 15

NO TURNOVERS
Starting Suits Osweiler, the Right Pick for Pats
By Paul Klee

He looked the part. And yes, that matters. It all matters.

On a Sunday to remember, Brock Osweiler turned 25, then he turned heads. On the sideline, after a stalled drive, he tracked down Demaryius Thomas, whom he had overthrown. Osweiler draped his long, capable arm over DT's shoulder and, patting his own chest like "my bad," took the blame for the misfire.

"He's a leader," running back C.J. Anderson said.

He sounded the part. Three-plus seasons behind Peyton Manning, who has never lost a press conference, and Osweiler clearly took notes. "I have not wasted a single day behind Peyton," he said. His clichéd, crafted answers after Denver's 17-15 win against the Bears at Soldier Field came straight from the school of Russell Wilson. (The Broncos drafted Osweiler ahead of Wilson way back when.) Lots of "run the football," "for the football team," and, finally, "at the end of the day." Nothing too flashy. Nothing to poke the Bears or Patriots. Osweiler at the podium — and a speech to his team a night before his first NFL start — felt entirely comfortable.

"It did not look like a guy in his first game out," coach Gary Kubiak said.

And Brock Nation should keep the part. That's the only sensible answer to the quarterback question facing Denver leading into a showdown against the Patriots.

Even if Manning's myriad injuries are magically healed, the Broncos should stick with the backup. Sorry, TV networks: Who's ready for Brady-Osweiler?

"I knew that (question) was coming," Kubiak said.

The coach remained noncommittal to the question that figures to shadow this season until it ends: Will it be the Sheriff, or the Deputy?

"Here's the deal…." Kubiak said, then added nothing.

Brock made his pitch. Under the towering shadows of the incomparable Chicago skyline, in a 20-degree wind chill that threatened to freeze over Lake Michigan by nightfall, against a former Denver quarterback who still hasn't learned it all matters, the Broncos stood tall behind their tall Montanan.

The Broncos don't need Osweiler to be Peyton Manning. They need him to not be Jay Cutler. When it was over, as he knotted his purple-plaid necktie and accessorized with purple dress socks, Osweiler was notable for what he didn't do: throw interceptions (zero), drop fumbles (zero), lose games (he's 1-0).

Wide receiver Cody Latimer celebrates his touchdown catch during the second half against the Chicago Bears. With the 17-15 win at Soldier Field, the Broncos got back on the winning track after two consecutive losses. (Associated Press)

"What we needed to do was go play clean football," Kubiak said.

Osweiler's line was conspicuous by what was absent: 20 of 27, 250 yards, two touchdown and … no turnovers. The Broncos played a game without a turnover for the first time. Cutler had two, and lost by two.

One fumble caromed to Malik Jackson ("I'm an honorary member of the 'No Fly Zone,'" he said); one interception sailed directly to Danny Trevathan.

"That's a good team, but I think we let it get away from us," the Bears quarterback said. "That's kind of been the story." (Forever.)

Of their future Hall of Famers who stayed back in Colorado, the Broncos missed DeMarcus Ware the most. Denver's quarterback controversy is alive and swell.

Smart money goes on Manning playing again. But it shouldn't be next week. A solid sports rule: Do what the opponent doesn't want you to do. The Dark Lord of Foxboro surely wants to face a quarterback who threw four interceptions last week.

"I was comfortable from the very first snap," Osweiler said.

Manning did not make the trip to Chicago, and it must be weird to watch his commercials during a Broncos game. It would be weirder if Brady-Manning Episode 17 (hey, that's Osweiler's number!) unfolds with him on the sideline. Manning is injured, and the scheming Patriots are a bad way to get healthy.

"Can't wait," T.J. Ward said of playing the Patriots, and not in New England.

The next quarterback era was delayed, the Broncos were delayed, Brock's parents were delayed.

Osweiler waited until his fourth season to get his first start. The Broncos waited on the team plane, for four-plus hours, thanks to a sudden snowstorm that turned the Windy City into a wild, winter wonderland.

"If we need to be delayed in the air more often, and circle airports, if that means wins, then sign me up for it," Osweiler said.

John and Kathy Osweiler's flight from Montana got canceled. His parents drove to Chicago. They wouldn't miss this.

Emerging from behind the quarterback curtain, their son delivered a speech to the team at its hotel. "It was about a mentality, the mentality I wanted us to play with today as a team," Osweiler recapped.

"Kind of, in a nutshell, it was him expressing his confidence in himself and our team: 'I got this. Don't worry about me. Let's all do our job. We'll get it done,'" veteran tight end Owen Daniels recalled.

This quarterback thing, it's more than arm strength and tight spirals. It's looking the part, sounding the part, playing the part.

"Ever since I started playing football I thought it was the quarterback's responsibility to be a leader of the football team," Osweiler said.

Against the Patriots, at least, the Wizard of Os should keep the part. ■

Broncos quarterback Brock Osweiler throws during the first half of the Broncos' close win. Osweiler had an efficient day passing the ball, with 250 yards, two touchdowns and no interceptions. (Associated Press)

NOVEMBER 29, 2015 • DENVER, COLORADO
BRONCOS 30, PATRIOTS 24, OT

BROCK ON
Wizard of Os Appears To Lock Up Starting Job
By Paul Klee

The course of Denver Broncos history shifted at 9:38 p.m. Brock Standard Time (BST). Time seemed to stop, along with 76,970 heartbeats. The moment felt so big, the crowd so hysterical, it was as if 9:39 shouldn't happen.

Brock Osweiler had 83 yards, a snowy swath of turf and the starting quarterback job of the Broncos in front of him. Oh, and Bill Belichick, in a hooded sweatshirt, to his right. They draw up dreams like this in Kalispell, Mont., where Osweiler learned good manners and how to toss a football. But even in a storybook a finish like this one would seem too unbelievable: Broncos 30, Patriots 24 (OT).

There's no going back now. The Broncos now are the Brockos.

Sunday night at Mile High was as much fun as you can have with seven layers of clothes on, and the Broncos found their quarterback of the future, and that future includes the next two months and the upcoming postseason.

What was the key indicator that suggested Osweiler is the man? Was it the throw to Demaryius Thomas that netted 36 yards on the critical scoring drive? Or the touchdown pass to Bubba Caldwell so perfectly placed it doubled as a handoff?

Neither. It was Osweiler changing a play at the line of scrimmage, a play that resulted in C.J. Anderson sprinting 48 yards for a walk-off touchdown run.

"It's a thing he saw. He made the change," Anderson said. "Next thing you know, the O-line did the rest. Touchdown."

Bedlam. Mayhem. Brockos Country.

"I put it in Brock's hands, actually," coach Gary Kubiak said.

Same with the quarterback job. If that seems coarse, it is. There's no nice way to replace a legend like Peyton Manning, no gentle way to move on from an era as successful as Manning's. The guy is one win away from the all-time record, for crying out loud. But can you envision a scenario in which that one win comes with the Broncos?

Osweiler took the job. He made Kubiak's and John Elway's decision an easy one.

Broncos brass learned it has a quarterback capable of succeeding Manning and beating the toughest weather conditions — snow and a wind

Broncos wide receiver Demaryius Thomas hauls in a 36-yard reception in front of the Patriots' Logan Ryan in the fourth quarter of Denver's 30-24 overtime win over New England. It was the only catch of the game for Thomas. (Mark Reis, The Gazette)

chill of 19 degrees, aka playoff weather — and the toughest opponent — the Patriots, who previously were 10-0.

And here's how Osweiler greeted media at the podium: "How's it going?"

Pretty decent, if you like 25-year-old quarterbacks who stare down the Dark Lord of Foxboro and don't flinch.

"I used to, as a kid in Montana, play in the backyard and play football in the winter," Osweiler said.

"If the receiver didn't catch it, it would go into a snowbank."

When the NFL schedule was released in the spring, Brady-Manning 17 on Nov. 29 jumped out on the marquee. It evolved into Brady-Brock 1, and it went to the kid.

Brady completed 23 of 42 pass attempts. So did Osweiler. The rest of the numbers sided with Brady. But the win sided with Osweiler.

"The one thing I do know is this was a tremendous team win," Osweiler said. "We couldn't win this football game if our defense didn't play the way they did."

Lots of things happened on a frigid night to shift football's plates, and an injury to New England star tight end Rob Gronkowski must list near the top. Depending on the severity of Gronk's injury — and it looked bad, as Gronkowski writhed in pain and Broncos and Patriots leaned on their helmets around him — the Super Bowl race was shuffled, flipped over and shaken into a puzzle no one can predict with any semblance of certainty. The AFC became anyone's game.

But the quarterback job of the Broncos?

That's an easy one.

Brock on. ■

Broncos wide receiver Emmanuel Sanders gathers in a 39-yard reception in the fourth quarter of Denver's big win over the rival Patriots. Sanders had a huge game with six catches for 113 yards. (Mark Reis, The Gazette)

Broncos quarterback Brock Osweiler runs for 3 yards on a fourth-and-one to give Denver a first down at the Patriots' 29-yard line during the first quarter. (Christian Murdock, The Gazette)

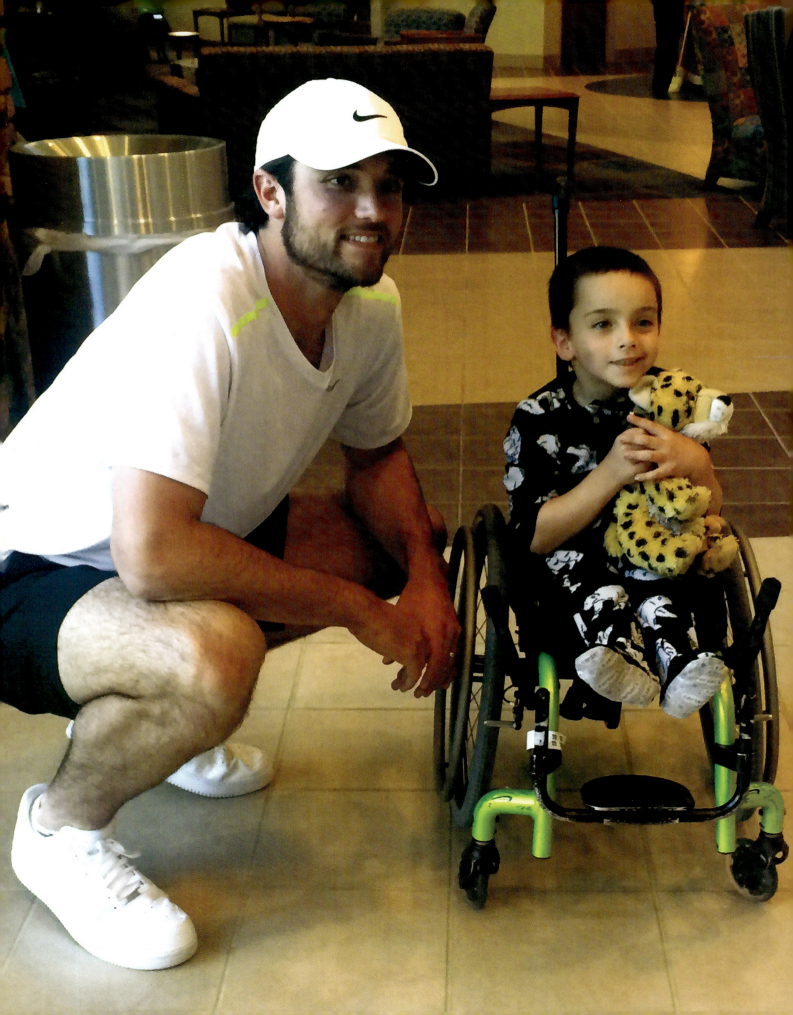

The Denver Broncos' 2015 Championship Season

BROCK OSWEILER
Breakout Broncos QB Brings Joy to Ailing Youths

By Paul Klee • December 6, 2015

Carter was 5 when he asked Amelia if she would be his girlfriend. She was 17. His charm and courage alone make Carter the coolest kid in Colorado. Wait, there's more.

Carter adores Peter Pan. Met him at Disneyland on Thursday, in fact, thanks to the Make-A-Wish Foundation. Sometimes he watches "Peter Pan" on a loop in his hospital room. It's even better when his parents, Dave and Jill, bring in the air mattress. "The air mattress means we're going to have a sleepover!" Carter says.

Carter is 6 now. He's not lived a single day without pain. He's had 29 surgeries. He's currently on 15 medications he must take daily. Carter has something called Caudal regression syndrome, a disorder that impacts just about everything below his belly button, his father says. Kidney, bladder, none of it works right. He was born here, at the Rocky Mountain Hospital for Children, and has spent large chunks of his life here. He has weekly checkups and lab work, three ER visits over the past five months. Heartbreaking, all of it.

And there's Carter, smiling.

"I love Legos," he says.

Sometimes I play Legos with my friend, Carter says.

"My friend plays football for the Broncos."

***

Amelia was 16 when her right leg began hurting. She was a high school junior, a setter for Rifle's volleyball team. Coaches thought Amelia could be all-conference for the Class 3A school. Maybe even play in college, if all went well.

Probably just shin splints, they figured. Cancer hides because it is a coward.

The chemotherapy treatments for Amelia's bone cancer forced her to miss her senior year of volleyball. She was in the midst of chemo when her friends picked her up to attend prom. She returned at midnight to find the hospital lobby decorated with balloons and a prom theme. She looked gorgeous, her mom says.

Amelia's room at the Rocky Mountain Hospital for Children was decorated like any teenage girl's should be, with posters of Demaryius Thomas, Eric

Brock Osweiler began visiting Carter two years ago. Carter, who is 6 now, has Caudal regression syndrome and has spent large parts of his life at the Rocky Mountain Hospital for Children and has had 29 surgeries. (Courtesy of the Denver Broncos)

Decker, Channing Tatum. She wore a Von Miller jersey on Sundays.

"I can never miss a game," she says.

Amelia's a middle child, our only daughter, says her mom, Debbie. Doctors found the tumor below her right knee, replaced 17 inches of her tibia with titanium. A volleyball fanatic, Amelia hasn't jumped since then. That's the goal when Amelia goes home for Christmas from her freshman year at Colorado Mesa.

She's studying to be a nurse. "It's what I've always wanted to do," she says.

Amelia had finished her final chemo treatment on Oct. 31 of last year. The family threw a party in her hospital room, so excited, her mom says, to be done with it.

That night Amelia cracked a fever of 104 degrees. It stayed for nine days. Doctors found spots in her lungs and feared the worst, that it was cancer again.

"Then this monster of a man walks in the room," her mom says.

Hi, Amelia. I'm Brock, he said.

"Here they are telling us she may have cancer in her lungs. I'm scared to death to lose my baby," Debbie says. "Then you have this man, this larger-than-life man, a man who plays football for the Broncos. And he's so real with her, and on the worst day of her life, he's making her smile. I mean, as her mom, how would you feel?"

***

Brock Osweiler was 23 when he met two friends he will have for the rest of their lives. He hadn't yet started a game for the Broncos, appeared on the cover of Sports Illustrated, opened SportsCenter after beating Tom Brady and the Patriots on a snowy night at Mile High.

Brock's 25 now and, right now in Colorado, larger than life.

To Carter, "He's my friend who plays football for the Broncos."

Used to be, Amelia and Carter would pass their hospital days by hanging out together, the two of them. Their rooms were across the hall. We'd have NERF gunfights, Amelia says. Carter tells all the nurses Amelia is his girlfriend.

I think Brock is more my age for a boyfriend, Amelia told Carter.

Absolutely not, Carter replied.

"I mean, what do you say to that? He's my favorite little kid in the world," Amelia says. "Of course I said yes."

Their circle grew by one. Brock plays Legos with Carter. He asks about Carter's Halloween costume. "I was Batman!" Carter says. They read books together. Carter stayed up to watch the Broncos-Patriots game until the pain meds kicked in.

"Brock, he just makes me happy," Carter says. "I feel happy when he's here. He's my friend."

I know. Grab another Kleenex.

"Carter is in a lot of pain. It's pretty much constant pain," says his mom, Jill. "To see him smile when Brock comes in the room, it does something to your heart."

When Amelia met Brock, she was in rough shape. He wore a gown and gloves to prevent infection. They talked Hunger Games. They talked volleyball. They talked Broncos. In the hospital room, her mom prayed: God, let her cry to him. Let her let it all out. She needs this.

"That was the first time she really opened up about her cancer," her mom says. "It was to Brock."

"He didn't talk to me about being sick and

Brock Osweiler regular visits Carter at Rocky Mountain Hospital for Children. "When you step into the children's hospital and see what those kids are going through, it reminds you that your bad days aren't really so bad," Osweiler said. "I'm playing a game. They're fighting for their life." (Courtesy of the Denver Broncos)

how I was feeling that day," Amelia says. "It was normal conversation about normal life stuff. He's just a good guy to talk to. It was really nice to have a friend like that."

I told Amelia and Carter I would say hi to Brock for them.

"Tell Brock I'm proud of him!" Carter said. He's 6.

"I love that kid," Brock said.

"Cancer shouldn't happen to anybody. But it definitely shouldn't happen to kids," he says. "They should be playing in the dirt, playing with their friends. When you see a kid like Carter, who's just so full of life despite what he's going through every day, it's pretty easy to stand by his side and support him.

"It just keeps life in perspective, you know? We're all so fortunate to be able to live our dreams on a daily basis. When you step into the children's hospital and see what those kids are going through, it reminds you that your bad days aren't really so bad. I'm playing a game. They're fighting for their life."

I met three heroes at the Rocky Mountain Hospital for Children.

One plays football for the Broncos. ■

DECEMBER 6, 2015 • SAN DIEGO, CALIFRONIA
BRONCOS 17, CHARGERS 3

WEST COASTING
Blueprint Is Evident: Manage and Damage
By Paul Klee

Stay Chargers, San Diego.

Don't leave. Don't abandon the loyal fans who lined the tunnel with bolts of passion Sunday. After yet another loss, the locals pleaded, "Great job, Orlando!" and "We love you, Philip!" and "Can I have your headband?" Don't succumb to the shifting plates of NFL relocation. Don't move to Los Angeles.

But if you must, don't change how you play football. Denver's 17-3 triumph at Qualcomm Stadium fit perfectly inside the box Gary Kubiak envisioned all along.

Angry, nasty defense. Mistake-free, nothing-flashy offense.

"I don't want to say 'manage,' but…." quarterback Brock Osweiler began.

Actually, yes, he did mean to say manage. That's his job, you know, and other than a careless, meaningless interception in the end zone, Osweiler managed his record to a 3-0 as the starter. And following that interception, Kubiak had the look of a father who wasn't mad, just disappointed. That's always way worse.

"As a quarterback and as an offense you want to score points every drive. You want to throw 50 times," Osweiler said. "But with the defense we have maybe that's not the best formula to win games as the Denver Broncos of 2015."

Kid Quarterback is a quick learner. The 2015 Broncos debuted their new Super Bowl formula in a beatdown by the beach.

The Chargers were a 51-yard field goal away from being shutout in what probably will be the Broncos' final trip to the cement relic that served as the site of their first Super Bowl title. And Brett Favre scored as many touchdowns Sunday as Rivers. Good things come in threes, and the Chargers managed only three, their fewest point total in this AFC West series since a 12-0 shutout in 1988.

"Three points too many," defensive lineman Derek Wolfe told me, with attitude.

"We're going to play to destroy people every week. That's what we want to do. We want to destroy people," Wolfe continued. "We have enough players and the right coaches to be the No. 1 defense in the league. Nothing else matters."

He's right, too. Colorado is Brocking like a hurricane over Osweiler, but the road back to California, for Super Bowl 50 in Santa Clara, is driven by the defense.

I must check the laws, but what the Broncos defense did to Rivers and the Chargers might be

Broncos wide receiver Demaryius Thomas, top, is tackled by Chargers inside linebacker Denzel Perryman during the second half of Denver's 17-3 win over San Diego. (Associated Press)

The Denver Broncos' 2015 Championship Season

illegal in Utah. The offense's job is simply to not mess it up.

Football is a foolish game, in a lot of ways, even if the bright sun and 78-degree temperature along the Pacific Ocean masked its dark side. On one series, two Chargers were carted off with injuries that could change their lives. Then I watched 6-foot-6, 330-pound lineman Chris Hairston half-spit, half-puke his way into the locker room. Brutal game, all of it.

The Broncos finished this one without seven starters due to injury (T.J. Ward, DeMarcus Ware, Sylvester Williams, Vernon Davis, C.J. Anderson, Danny Trevathan and, yes, Peyton Manning). But it's not an overly complicated game, for the Broncos. Commit fewer turnovers than the opponent, no one has been able to beat them (6-0). Doesn't get simpler than that.

"How many catches did (Chargers wide receiver) Stevie Johnson have today?" Chris Harris Jr. asked.

Zero, I said, as if Harris didn't already know.

"That's what we do," Harris said. "We're the No. 1 defense for a reason."

In an obnoxious postgame locker room, the Broncos defense hollered like it was the baddest in all the land. Aqib Talib shouted, "(Gosh) damn, No Fly Zone!" Malik Jackson thanked Broncos Country for its attendance. Harris asked for other various stats, too.

But it hasn't always been sunshine and seashells between the offense and the defense. After the Chiefs flipped four interceptions into a 29-13 win at Mile High, the defense, which adores its own stats, grew restless with Manning's offense.

You prefer this approach, correct?

"You see what happens when a team has to travel 70, 80 yards. It's tough for teams to do that," Harris said.

The three games since the Kansas City loss have been nothing short of a bonding experience. David Bruton had 12 tackles (and limped through the locker room with a bum knee), Trevathan scored a pick-6, and Von Miller sacked Rivers twice. Vonnie Football and Phrustrated Philip exchanged holiday greetings, too.

"I don't think he liked the cologne I was wearing," Miller explained.

"Oh, Philip? He had some good lines today," Talib said. "He always does."

Just as Coors Field becomes Chicago East for a Cubs series, Qualcomm was Colorado West on Sunday. The stadium was crushed in orange. The Chargers, forever sweet hosts, flashed highlights of Philadelphia's 35-28 win at New England, a result that shoved the Broncos into the No. 2 seed in the AFC, for the time being.

"Did they lose?" Talib said, as if he didn't know.

"Now we get to control our own destiny," Talib said. "We win out we get to stay at home."

Kicking and screaming is so September. By the sea, the Broncos could see their new Super Bowl blueprint: Manage and damage.

"Eventually we're going to come out with a turnover," Harris said. "If the offense can continue to not give away the ball and play smart, punts are good for us."

Nothing else matters, they said. ■

Broncos running back C.J. Anderson, top, rushes over Chargers cornerback Steve Williams during the first half. (Associated Press)

DECEMBER 13, 2015 • DENVER, COLORADO
RAIDERS 15, BRONCOS 12

STRUGGLE
Thomas Will Return to Form, and so Will Broncos
By David Ramsey

Demaryius Thomas stood in front of a small crowd at his locker. His voice was turned down extra low. His left shoulder was bleeding. His mind was quick to explain how the Broncos found a way to lose to the Raiders, 15-12.

"You kind of want to point at the offense because they didn't play their best," Thomas said. Notice he said "they" instead of "we."

But Thomas isn't dodging responsibility. He realizes where tens of thousands of Broncos will be pointing this week. They'll be pointing at No. 88.

Thomas failed to hang on to a touchdown in the dying seconds of the first half and fumbled in the third quarter and completed his hat trick of horrors by dropping a vital pass in the fourth quarter.

The last drop hurt the most.

Brock Osweiler placed the ball squarely in Thomas' hands. He was alone. It was the most basic of football plays.

The ball slipped from his hands, ending a Broncos drive, and he walked slowly away. It's become a ritual. Thomas shaking his head while enraged, baffled fans toss objects at their TVs.

"It can become mental a little," Thomas said, explaining the drops. "I've been doing this awhile, and I just got to put it on myself and make the play."

His storyline for the day came so close to being entirely different. Thomas has usually been sensational since 2012, collecting 28 100-yard games and 5,455 yards.

But he's struggled to get into rhythm with Osweiler. Thomas delivered a monster game against the Packers on Nov. 1, catching 11 Peyton Manning passes for 168 yards.

He hasn't topped the 100-yard mark since.

Even with all his struggles, Thomas caught 10 passes for 95 yards against the Raiders. If he hadn't dropped the TD pass and hadn't fumbled and hadn't dropped the fourth-quarter pass, he's a hero standing in front of his locker explaining victory instead of defeat.

Explaining a single NFL game is a difficult dance. There's always the temptation to go apocalyptic after a defeat and say the Broncos exposed themselves as impostors.

Yes, the Broncos' offense refused endless chances to win the game. Osweiler declined to avoid this obvious point, repeatedly saying it's his job to deliver touchdowns instead of field goals.

And then there's the temptation to sweep away a single loss and look at the big picture.

Broncos wide receiver Demaryius Thomas is stopped at the two-yard line following a 17-yard reception in the second quarter. (Mark Reis, The Gazette)

I believe these Broncos were best revealed this season in their beatdown of the Packers and their dramatic comeback against the Patriots. This remains, despite Sunday's pitiful offensive effort, one of the NFL's top four teams. A Super Bowl journey remains possible, if not quite probable.

Thomas will return to being Thomas. He's in a long slump, but he'll develop better chemistry with Osweiler and again make routine catches along with the soaring grabs that test the limits of imagination.

On Sunday, tight end Owen Daniels offered the only reliable hands for Osweiler. Daniels knows it's not always that way.

He's a survivor of days filled with drops.

"It's all in your head," Daniels said. "It's all mental when guys happen to drop some balls that are right in their lap. That happens."

Daniels glanced to his right and saw Thomas standing a few lockers away.

"DT is one of the best players I've ever played with," Daniels said.

"If you keep talking about it and keep harping on it, that doesn't help you catch passes."

Every season offers a series of crises. The current crisis is No. 88's suddenly slippery hands.

Thomas, now talking to an audience of one, lowered his voice to a near whisper.

"You can't let them bother you," Thomas said of his drops. "You can't think about them … or you're going to have another mistake."

That's true. Catching a football is similar to many tasks in life. The harder you try, the higher chance of failure. Thomas is a natural who earns $14 million per season to outbattle and outleap defensive backs.

The DT crisis will soon end. ■

Receiver Demaryius Thomas is chased by Raider defenders Malcolm Smith, left, and Leon Orr on a 17-yard reception in the second quarter. (Mark Reis, The Gazette)

The Denver Broncos' 2015 Championship Season

DECEMBER 20, 2015 • PITTSBURGH, PENNSYLVANIA
STEELERS 34, BRONCOS 27

STEEL RESOLVE
Denver Fails to Score in Second Half for Third Game
By Paul Klee

This wasn't Brock's fault. He said afterward it was, but he's just being a good teammate. John and Kathy Osweiler didn't raise a meanie in Montana.

I suppose you could frame it that way, as Brock's fault, if it helps, or if there's a Peyton Manning jersey wrapped and waiting beneath the Christmas tree.

But the reason the Broncos should return to the Manning era — whenever he's healthy, of course — actually has nothing to do with Osweiler.

It's not because Brock's Broncos offense went scoreless in the second half of Sunday's 34-27 loss to the Steelers, just as it went scoreless in the second half of the previous two games.

It's not because Osweiler threw a regrettable interception that turned Heinz Field's Terrible Towels from hand warmers into helicopters, or completed only 7 of 26 passes after halftime, or because it feels like he's under siege on every snap.

No, the Broncos must go back to Manning, if that foot is healed, because there's a $15 million quarterback on the sideline of a team that's paid to win now.

You do it because, as Osweiler said himself, the kid is still learning to play the position.

"I think it's a big learning curve for me to decide when to take off, when to throw it down the field, and when it's time to throw it away," Osweiler said at the podium.

It's not his fault, but late December, with a playoff berth suddenly in doubt, is no time for learning.

It's time for winning, and no one has won more games than Manning.

You do it because maybe, just maybe, the same jolt of life Osweiler injected into the Broncos in the Patriots game could be replicated in Manning's inevitable return.

"The thing is, we still have our goals to reach," said Emmanuel Sanders, a bright spot on a dark day with 181 receiving yards. "We can still make the playoffs. We can still win the Super Bowl."

At night, with city lights sinking into the Allegheny River, this city is beautiful. In the first half, with four touchdowns by Osweiler, the Broncos' offense was beautiful.

Down 17 points, the record crowd of 66,234 might've considered throwing in their Towels. But let's talk about that second half, again.

"We got our (butts) kicked. Straight (butt) whooping," running back C.J. Anderson told me in a dazed locker room. "That was the difference."

Linebacker Von Miller celebrates after the Broncos stopped the Steelers on a fourth and five late in the fourth quarter. The Steelers ultimately prevailed, 34-27. (Christian Murdock, The Gazette)

If you haven't seen the new Star Wars, Sunday night offered a glimpse.

Antonio Brown is a Jedi Knight. There's no other explanation for how he mind-tricked Chris Harris Jr., who hadn't allowed a touchdown catch since Week 12 of the 2013 season and saw Brown skywalk to 16 catches and 189 yards.

Brown isn't the best offensive player the Broncos have faced this season; he's the best they've faced the past three seasons.

"If you play this game long enough, you're going to get your tail kicked more than once," said Brown, the first in NFL history with two games of at least 15 catches.

"They (Denver's offense) did enough. They scored enough points," Harris said. "That's on the defense. We should've won the game."

The Steelers haven't won a playoff game in five years, but, in basketball terms, will be the mid-major nobody wants to see in the postseason tournament.

Foam fingers crossed they go to New England, or Kansas City, or anywhere but Colorado.

Prior to kickoff, Manning circled the field with autographs, ignoring only the fans who offered a Terrible Towel to sign. (Hey, a man's got to have standards.)

He chatted up Osweiler on the sideline after the interception and in the locker room after the game. Manning did most of the talking. Osweiler listened, and learned.

Again, and it deserves repeating: Osweiler is 3-2 as the starter, with matchups against Denver's former offensive coordinator (who knows him well), Denver's former defensive coordinator (who knows him well), Denver's former head coach (who knows him really well), Bill Belichick and a Steelers squad that would have needed a Christmas miracle to make the playoffs with a loss.

Don't ignore the part where Demaryius Thomas and Vernon Davis forgot how to catch. DT will snap out of it, always does.

Davis seems more interested in reading his Twitter mentions than risking a big hit, a chiseled figure who so far has been more style than substance.

The Broncos are not kicking and screaming. They are fumbling and bumbling and threatening to blow their own house down.

That's two straight games the Broncos choked away double-digit leads, and the Chiefs are breathing fire down their neck.

"I think there were some plays we should have made by a lot of people, not just the quarterback," coach Gary Kubiak said.

The kid's going to be all right, but Brock Standard Time (BST) should restart next season.

Manning has practiced exactly twice in a month, and there's hardly a guarantee he can relocate the mojo of touchdowns past.

But if you go down, you go down with the Hall of Famer, and I suspect that's what Kubiak and John Elway will do.

"We had two good days of practice last week," Kubiak said. "We'll start over this week and see where we are at."

Need a hug?

Here's one, wrapped in a steel bow: The Broncos lost here, at the intersection of three rivers, in December 1997. They lost two games that December, actually. Then they won the Super Bowl. They lost two games in December the following year, too. Then they won another Super Bowl.

OK, that's enough holiday cheer. As the final horn buzzed the Broncos back to reality, a train rumbled from across the river.

Safe to assume it carried coal. ■

Peyton Manning looks on from the sideline during the first half of the Broncos' December 20 loss at Pittsburgh. (Associated Press)

DECEMBER 28, 2015 • DENVER, COLORADO
BRONCOS 20, BENGALS 17, OT

BY HOOK OR BY CROOK
Broncos Prevail Again
By Paul Klee

They don't go quietly, do they? Cut off their foot, or their left tackle, and the Broncos throw it right back at you. They don't have nine lives. They have 12.

Here it was again, the Broncos smelling like Greeley, and what do you know?

They won, 20-17 in overtime, against the Cincinnati Bengals, when their chances of doing so appeared frozen solid. That makes three AFC playoff teams who have witnessed their late-game magic firsthand: Kansas City (on a fumble return with seconds left), New England (in overtime, and the snow) and Cincinnati (after erasing a 14-0 deficit Monday night). When hearts beat the loudest, when palms sweat the sweatiest, they get 'er done. Again and again and again.

That makes 12 of their 15 games decided in the final five minutes of regulation or in overtime. And the Broncos are now 3-0 in overtime. How's your heart doing?

Take away their water, the Broncos don't mind chugging rain.

It's OK to be real about it. Chances are, the Broncos aren't going anywhere in the postseason. Too many issues on the offensive line, too green at quarterback, too many trips to Foxboro probably looming. We're all friends here. We can agree.

But if your favorite team is the Patriots, Chiefs or Bengals, do you want to be in a one-possession game with the season on the line? The Broncos do things when they shouldn't.

The Broncos clinched a playoff spot Monday night in front of 74,511 hooligans with orange in their blood and icicles in their nosehairs. The temp at kickoff? Sixteen degrees, and only two home games in Broncos history have been colder.

When the Broncos defense — oh, the Broncos defense — ended a memorable, frigid night by recovering a fumble with 9:42 on the overtime clock, C.J. Anderson hopped and skipped and jumped into the tunnel. Danny Trevathan yanked off his sweaty (or was it frozen solid?) headband and tossed it into Section 135. The loudest crowd I've seen the past four seasons at Mile High, and there have been a few, danced a giddy dance, knowing the Broncos can clinch a top-two seed and a playoff bye by beating San Diego.

After that? Who knows? This season suggests whatever it is won't be boring.

The Broncos are flawed in so many places.

Running back C.J. Anderson rushes the field before scoring a touchdown in the fourth quarter. Anderson's score put the Broncos in the lead. (Stacie Scott, The Gazette)

From the second half at Pittsburgh to the first half against Cincinnati, they were outscored 35-3. They had not scored a second-half offensive touchdown in December until they scored two against the Bengals.

The score was 7-0, then it was 14-0. The Bengals converted four straight third downs, then five straight, then six straight, then seven straight.

The Broncos' defense allowed 16 first downs in the first half. The Broncos' defense had played six entire games without allowing more than 16 first downs.

They didn't fold, or stumble. They accelerated.

"That's what this league is about, is finding out what you're about," coach Gary Kubiak said.

In Montana cold that must have felt like home, and with a bum left shoulder that took a major wallop in the first quarter, 25-year-old quarterback Brock Osweiler finished regulation with 23 of 29 passing for 262 yards and a passer rating of 115.8.

Osweiler didn't wear a coat on the sideline, and the Broncos couldn't protect him from the Bengals' elements.

The Associated Press reported 100,000 people moved to Colorado this year. None play offensive line?

The Broncos had to dig deep for this one. Cheesy, and true.

Maybe it's because they've been down so often, stuck in tight corners on so many Sundays (and now Mondays). They know the path to light. It's tough to make a case they are decidedly better than any of the teams who will qualify for the postseason in the AFC.

But they are in the playoffs, yet again, and when it's time to go quietly, they kick and scream as if their pride's on the line. ■

Broncos running back C.J. Anderson heads for the end zone in the fourth quarter of the Broncos' 20-17 overtime win. (Jerilee Bennett, The Gazette)

THE DENVER BRONCOS' 2015 CHAMPIONSHIP SEASON

JANUARY 3, 2016 • DENVER, COLORADO
BRONCOS 27, CHARGERS 20

MAN, OH MANNING
Denver Grabs AFC's No. 1 Seed; Who Is No. 1 QB?
By Paul Klee

We dwell in the early days of 2016, not the early days of 2006. This truth is the prime reason why healthy, youthful Brock Osweiler should start as Broncos quarterback over creaky, ancient Peyton Manning.

Yes, I realize Manning played a role in the thrilling second-half comeback of the Broncos' needlessly dramatic 27-20 victory over the Chargers. Please be sure to note he played a minor role.

"I can't take credit for having a really good handoff," Manning said.

Exactly.

The Broncos offense awoke in the third quarter and realized they were playing the Chargers, a team with four wins in 15 games. After this awakening, Ronnie Hillman and C.J. Anderson carried the Broncos to the No. 1 seed in the AFC playoffs. Manning was a supporting actor in the revival. He wasn't the star.

A week ago, Osweiler delivered a superlative, clutch second half to rescue the Broncos against the Bengals. Earlier, he conquered the Patriots. He's at his best against the best.

Manning?

Ah, do you remember Manning's last playoff performance, or should I say disappearance? A year ago, on a quiet night at Mile High, Manning was the prime reason the Broncos stumbled to a playoff loss to the Colts. His arm lacked might. He struggled with decisions and timing as his greatness embarked on a permanent journey to the past tense.

Nostalgia is always powerful. I understand the temptation to embrace sentiment and ignore the ravages of time. This temptation led Muhammad Ali to fight far too long and Michael Jordan to plod along as a pitiful imitation of Michael Jordan. Manning is fragile, cursed with a surgically repaired neck and a gimpy left foot.

Manning has said he will do anything to help this edition of the Broncos win the Super Bowl. Anything should be laboring as a 39-year-old backup.

Osweiler's excellence as the Broncos' starter continued in the first half against the Chargers. He passed for 222 yards and was on pace to throw for 400. He placed a pass directly into Jordan Norwood's hands and watched it bounce into the arms of the Chargers Steve Williams. Another interception came after he was assaulted by linebacker Melvin Ingram in the pocket.

"I don't really think Brock was having any troubles," Manning said. "I thought Brock was

Peyton Manning throws downfield against the Chargers. Manning entered the game in the third quarter and lead the Broncos to a 27-20 win over the Chargers in the final game of the regular season. (Christian Murdock, The Gazette)

making good throws."

But after Anderson fumbled on the Broncos' first drive of the third quarter, coach Gary Kubiak told Osweiler he was done for the day.

Manning was coming to the rescue.

Hillman turned to see Manning taking snaps on the sideline. He saw Osweiler wearing a cap. He knew what was ahead.

"I was surprised," Hillman said. "I wasn't expecting Peyton to come in. Listen, I was just as surprised as ya'll was."

Nothing in sport carries quite the disruptive potential of a quarterback controversy. The Manning vs. Osweiler battle will begin a statewide discussion/argument. Families will divide. Friendships will teeter. Shouting will be common.

This is, no doubt, going to be a lot of fun.

Osweiler, who has a bad habit of not saying anything when he talks, swears he will be content regardless of Kubiak's decision.

"As long as this football team is winning games, shoot, I don't care who is playing quarterback," Osweiler said.

Yeah, sure, Brock.

Cornerback Bradley Roby was more frank. He believes the selection is, using his word, "obviously" Peyton for the playoffs.

"He's back," Roby said. "He didn't look like he was hurting. He led us to victory. You have to play him."

Tight end Owen Daniels walked a more evasive route. He emphasized his respect and "love" for Osweiler and Manning.

So, which quarterback should start?

"I don't have a vote," Daniels said, his voice rising. "I don't have a vote, man."

That's not true. Roby votes for Manning. I vote for Osweiler. Daniels keeps his ballot secret. We all have a vote. But only one vote matters. Kubiak soon will decide which quarterback he will entrust with the rest of this hugely entertaining and just as confusing Broncos season.

It's 2016, not 2006. Kubiak must go with Osweiler. ■

Demaryius Thomas heads for the end zone on a 72-yard touchdown catch and run. (Mark Reis, The Gazette)

The Denver Broncos' 2015 Championship Season

PEYTON MANNING
Let's Applaud Legend Before Exit

By David Ramsey • January 27, 2016

As Peyton Manning drags his gimpy left foot and his surgically repaired neck on a gallant quest to rule football, only a person who lacks a beating heart would refuse to applaud as No. 18 approaches His Final Hurrah.

I have a heart.

Manning seeks to defy the aging process and his tortured postseason history. After an abominable playoff performance last season against the Colts, he refused to surrender. After tossing 17 interceptions in the first nine games this season, he refused again.

I told my children, early and often, to follow Winston Churchill's advice: "Never, never, never quit." Each time Manning waddles on the field, he towers as a profile in courage. He refused to be conquered by pain and doubt and skeptics and snarling defenders and a massive man from Montana named Brock Osweiler.

I was one of the skeptics. After Osweiler led the Broncos to a 4-2 record against exceedingly tough competition, I believed No. 17 had passed Manning as the obvious choice to lead the Broncos into the playoffs. Coach Gary Kubiak chose No. 18. He went with the experienced and sentimental choice.

Kubiak's choice was supported by the masses. Trust me on that one. I've heard from several dozen Gazette readers who question my support for Osweiler.

They keep asking: "What do you have against Peyton?"

Answer: Nothing.

He's one of the top-five quarterbacks of all time. He led the revival of a franchise that had been mutilated during the brief reign of Josh "The Boy Blunder" McDaniels. He brings football's most beautiful mind to every huddle.

Age is the sole reason for my doubts about Manning. Joe Montana never took a snap at age 39. Neither did Troy Aikman or Joe Namath or Terry Bradshaw. They were sitting in easy chairs at this point in their lives. Old man Manning will soon tangle with 300-pound linemen.

We all watched Nov. 15 as Manning threw four interceptions against the Chiefs. Just over two months ago, Manning looked ancient and spent and done. He looked every minute of his 39 years.

Manning, in yet another comeback, silenced

Peyton Manning looks to throw in the first half of the Broncos' 29-13 loss to the Kansas City Chiefs on November 15. After completing just five passes against the Chiefs, Mannning sat out the Broncos' next six games. (Mark Reis, The Gazette)

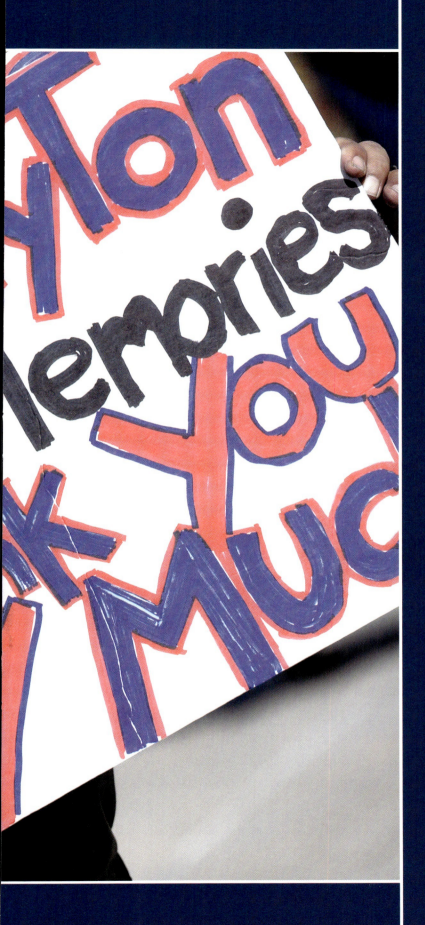

his skeptics this January. He hopes for a final silencing at his fourth Super Bowl. John Elway delivered the finest career finale in football history when he led the Broncos to a Super Bowl win over Dan Reeves and the Atlanta Falcons on Feb. 1, 1999. Manning can equal this ultimate exit with a win in Santa Clara.

It's easy to argue Osweiler would have taken the Broncos to the Super Bowl. It's easy to argue because a ferocious, arrogant, stingy group of defenders carries this team. Manning led the offense to 43 points in playoff struggles with the Steelers and Patriots. Osweiler's offense placed 57 points (with the aid of one overtime) against the same two teams.

But any talk about Osweiler is only speculation. In the realm of reality, Manning directed the Broncos to Super Bowl 50. He was seldom spectacular. He was almost always steady.

Not everyone is rooting for No. 18. The state of North Carolina, along with wide sections of the South, hope His Final Hurrah is a bust.

But the vast majority of the Land of the Free wants this classy, stubborn, meticulous, courageous quarterback to limp into his football sunset with a victory.

On Saturday morning, I was driving along Broadway, a few blocks from the Denver home where my parents raised five children and even more dachshunds. My parents were Bronco fans, as in fanatics. Family dogs were named "Smith" and "Atwater." Mom talked about Elway as if he were her son. Dad paced the TV room, unable to sit during the final, tense minutes of Bronco games.

As I drove the wide boulevard, a billboard grabbed my eye. It read: "No Matter What, Thank You Peyton." ■

Noby Gomez brought a tribute to The King and Peyton Manning for the Broncos' January 3 game against the San Diego Chargers. (Mark Reis, The Gazette)

Peyton Manning walks off the field after the Broncos defeated the Chargers 27-20 in the final game of the 2015 season. (Christian Murdock, The Gazette)

AFC DIVISIONAL PLAYOFF
JANUARY 17, 2016 • DENVER, COLORADO
BRONCOS 23, STEELERS 16

DRAGGING IT OUT
Broncos' Latest like Prequels — Ugly, Magical
By Paul Klee

Quentin Tarantino will direct it. No, he swears too much.

Scorsese? Eastwood? Let's go with Spielberg to direct the film about this Broncos season, if it rolls on, through the New England Patriots, into Super Bowl 50.

Because the whole thing feels like a movie, doesn't it? Lead quarterback goes down, comes back to win a divisional playoff game. Defense looks average, returns to force the key turnover, over and over. The only guarantee is drama befitting of Hollywood. Seventeen stanzas so far, the next more spooky than the last.

"Starting with the first one, right?" Peyton Manning said after the Broncos somehow beat the Steelers, 23-16, in front of 76,956 cast members at Mile High.

Now for the climactic scene. It was always hovering in the background as a possibility, a shootout pitting good vs. evil (depending on your area code): Brady vs. Manning, one more time, for a 17th time. The Broncos host the Patriots in the AFC Championship Game, because of course they do.

"Couldn't have it no better way," former Pat Aqib Talib said afterward in the locker room. "The only way to go to the Super Bowl is to go through them."

How does it end? That's where an imaginative director comes in. Think of the most fantastical, far-fetched, unlikely conclusion and that's how it ends. That's the only way the Broncos know how to end it. They've won 10 games by a touchdown or less, swiping victory from the jaws of defeat so often it's become the usual.

Is it Manning limping down the field for a game-winning touchdown in the final minute? Is it Tom Brady, who is 2-6 at Sports Authority Field, leading the Patriots on a 20-point comeback in the fourth quarter? Or is it Bill Belichick dumping the hoodie and opting for a three-piece suit to complement his scowl?

At this point, anything's possible. The Broncos choose their own adventure and make the audience as uncomfortable as possible until the credits roll.

"We've kind of won all kinds of different ways," coach Gary Kubiak said.

The Broncos advanced to their 10th AFC championship game and ninth under Pat Bowlen's ownership, tying Bowlen with Patriots owner Robert Kraft.

But this one is not like the others. To appreciate

Bennie Fowler runs past the Steelers for a first down on the winning drive in the fourth quarter. (Christian Murdock, The Gazette)

The Denver Broncos' 2015 Championship Season

these Broncos is to embrace the ugly and wait for the beauty. This time it arrived in the form of Bradley Roby stripping the ball away from Steelers tailback Fitzgerald Toussaint, a fumble that bounced in the general direction of DeMarcus Ware. He smothered the ball and breathed new life into a manic crowd that stood on its feet for the entire fourth quarter, waiting for That One Play that always seems to come. It did again.

It wasn't looking good up until that point, but does it ever? Sometimes with this team — most times — the first half doesn't even matter. "We're just trying to survive, man," Malik Jackson said.

They are a team only a Broncos fanatic could love. They won a playoff game by scoring one offensive touchdown in a season when they won a game by scoring zero offensive touchdowns. Their beauty is in the eye of the late Barrel Man.

How fitting their biggest play was one in which their 39-year-old quarterback fell to the ground. Manning, untouched, took a self-sack. Then he rose to complete a pass to Emmanuel Sanders for 34 yards. You can't make these things up.

"I don't really want to analyze that play too much," Manning said with a smile. "I kind of just want it to go away."

Manning was right, too. This all started with the first one, Week 1 against the Ravens, a last-minute interception that sealed a win. They did it again in Week 2, a win at Kansas City, and eight more times the Broncos won a game by a touchdown or less. This is what they do. They don't die. They fight and kick and scream and do all the things your JV basketball coach told you to do, things that just seemed like something old people say but actually are the only proven avenue to success. They keep working.

Wide receiver Demaryius Thomas carries the ball for a 2-point conversion in the fourth quarter. (Jerilee Bennett, The Gazette)

The Denver Broncos' 2015 Championship Season

"We're going to play football until the clock says 0:00," Talib said.

They did it in a playoff game, one the Broncos trailed from 1:22 in the first until C.J. Anderson squeaked across the goal line with 3:00 left in the fourth.

If a lost soul had snuck into Sports Authority Field to see these Broncos for the first time, they might consider it to be the most nerve-racking game they've seen this season. And I don't think it would crack the top five this season.

If anyone is expecting 350 passing yards and four touchdowns from Manning in the AFC Championship Game, they will be disappointed. If they expect a tight game that stops hearts into the fourth quarter, that's more like it. These aren't the Super Bowl-winning Broncos that blasted opponents with Terrell Davis, or the Manning teams that scored 30 points before your second beer, or even Jake Plummer's Broncos who reached an AFC Championship Game before losing to these same Steelers.

The Broncos are where they are because it hasn't been easy. They stand on the brink of another Super Bowl because they had the gumption to erase late deficits against playoff teams like the Steelers, Chiefs, Bengals and, yes, the Patriots.

"I've never been part of a team that handles adversity so well," Von Miller said.

The movie's not over yet. Brady's got that Hollywood thing going. He can play himself.

Next question is, who plays Manning? ■

Peyton Manning smiles as he leaves the field following Denver's 23-16 win over Pittsburgh. (Christian Murdock, The Gazette)

The Denver Broncos' 2015 Championship Season

GETTING PHYSICAL
Broncos Defense Changed Soft Reputation in 2015
By Paul Klee • January 12, 2016

It was an innocuous question, tossed at one of the most levelheaded guys in the locker room, Broncos safety Darian Stewart.

What was Denver's reaction to Pittsburgh lineman Cody Wallace leveling David Bruton Jr. with a shot to the head in their Week 15 matchup?

"Mad. Some BS," Stewart told The Gazette. "(No.) 72, we already know. We've got his number."

That bubbling sound is bad blood boiling over. Days after unsportsmanlike conduct sent the Bengals home and nudged the Steelers into a playoff game at Denver, the bottom line for Broncos-Steelers became crystal clear: They aren't going to play nice. The team that advances to the AFC title game will be the one that delivers the hardest hits, while also keeping its head when tempers flare.

Can the Broncos be the smarter and tougher team?

For the Broncos, it's also the perfect opportunity, against the perfect opponent, to dispel their reputation as a finesse outfit that doesn't like to be pushed around. In the first three years of the Peyton Manning era, the Broncos were viewed through a lens of pretty offense and Star Wars numbers. Playoff losses to the Ravens, Seahawks and Colts shared a commonality: Punch 'em. They won't punch back.

"We feel like we let them get back in the game," Pro Bowl cornerback Aqib Talib said of Pittsburgh's 34-27 win. "We're all looking forward to seeing them again."

The Broncos watched Saturday night as the Bengals imploded in the fourth quarter of Pittsburgh's win. Cincinnati linebacker Vontaze Burfict turned to brawn when time and score called for brains. Burfict's dome shot on Antonio Brown drew a 15-yard unnecessary roughness penalty that put the Steelers in line for a game-winning field goal. I asked Broncos lineman Malik Jackson for his takeaway.

"What I learned from it is you've got to keep your composure. I think Cincinnati had the game; they just lost their composure," Jackson said. "We learned a lot. Watch your composure. Coaches don't get on the field. Everybody do your part. Don't be selfish. Don't make it all about you."

Oh, the Steelers weren't sinless. They rarely are. Linebacker Ryan Shazier delivered a dangerous shot on Cincinnati's Giovani Bernard that knocked the

Cornerback Aqib Talib breaks up a pass to the Steelers' Martavis Bryant in the January 17 AFC Divisional playoff 23-16 win. The Broncos avenged a 34-27 regular season loss to the Steelers. (Jerilee Bennett, The Gazette)

running back from the game. Any notion the Steelers, a club that has employed beacons of sportsmanship Hines Ward and James Harrison, are victims of dirty football is rich. What's next, the Spurs complaining about too much flopping?

But the Broncos' defense has built a similar reputation of its own. Eye pokes are still outlawed, and Denver often walks a thin line between physical football and over-the-line antics. Here's a hunch Sunday at Sports Authority Field will feature a quick whistle as the officiating crew attempts to get an early hold on the game.

By my count, the Broncos during the regular season were penalized 290 yards more than their opponents. The Steelers were penalized 281 yards less than their opponents. Pittsburgh drew 12 flags for unnecessary roughness. Denver drew 11 of those flags. Yes, this figures to be a rough one.

"We just know what it is now," Stewart said. "We just know it's going to be a physical game. You can pretty much count on that."

One incident remains stuck in Denver's side: Wallace's cheap shot on Bruton. Over the course of a drama-filled Broncos season, no other play lit tempers on their sideline like Wallace torpedoing Bruton. Plus, it happened only three weeks ago.

Wallace reportedly earned a $23,152 fine. The Broncos pleaded for a suspension that never came. A fourth-round pick who climbed the NFL ladder from special teams ace to team captain, Bruton is one of the most popular players in the locker room. As the longest-tenured Bronco on the roster, Bruton is their Ferris Bueller: the linemen, safeties, linebackers, cornerbacks, quarterbacks, wide receivers, running backs, tight ends — they think he's a righteous dude.

Aqib Talib tackles Chargers wide receiver Javontee Herndon short of a first down. (Christian Murdock, The Gazette)

"We were very un-pleased about the hit. We thought some more action should have been brought to the guy," Jackson said. "We thought it was a dirty hit. But now you know what to look out for, who to look out for, what to do."

Are the Broncos preparing as if Ben Roethlisberger (shoulder) and Antonio Brown (concussion) are going to play Sunday?

"Ben will be there. AB will be there. We want them to be there," Talib said. "If we didn't want them to be there, that means I want AB to be messed up. That's a good dude. That's a good family dude. We don't want him to be messed up."

Roethlisberger and Brown wrecked the Broncos, combining for 16 catches, 189 receiving yards and two touchdowns. Saturday at Cincinnati, they also combined for a pair of injuries that could impact their mobility Sunday.

I asked Jackson, a linemen enjoying a career year, if defensive players take note when an opponent has an ailing body part such as Roethlisberger's shoulder.

"You just try to get to him faster. Since Ben's probably going to be hurt a little bit, we'll probably get some quicker passes, some more screens and things like that," Jackson said. "We've just got to get our hands up. When he does hold it, we've got to get to him, if not lay on him. Just hit him. We've got to hit him. That's all there is."

Did I mention the Broncos committed a season-high 12 penalties in the game at Pittsburgh, or that the Steelers drew nine flags, one shy of their season high?

Leave the handshakes and man hugs at home. This isn't going to be pretty.

Turning the other cheek will be Denver's best move. ■

Defenders Aqib Talib and Chris Harris Jr. stop Julian Edelman short of a first down on a fourth-and-one. The Broncos defeated the Patriots 20-18 in the AFC Championship game. (Mark Reis, The Gazette)

AFC CHAMPIONSHIP
JANUARY 24, 2016 • DENVER, COLORADO
BRONCOS 20, PATRIOTS 18

MILE HIGH CELEBRATION
Every Man Gave All During Improbable Run
By Paul Klee

This is what you will read the most: Peyton Manning will be the oldest quarterback to start in a Super Bowl. Be forewarned, the age thing is still a thing.

If only America would identify with how Manning celebrated on a glorious, sun-soaked Sunday, it could see what these Broncos, and this man, are really about. His party was muted, in the background. As the Denver Broncos accepted the Lamar Hunt trophy as champions of the AFC, Manning crouched on the edge of an aluminum platform layered in glitter and giddiness. He watched.

In that telling moment, Manning looked like he sought the spotlight about as much as Tom Brady sought another encounter with Von Miller. Here, let his Dad tell it, because Dad always tells it better: "It's been a long year. He's hung in there with a lot of young guys, a young team, and he gets to join them in the Super Bowl. I think that's what it's about to him," Archie Manning said in a quiet hallway underneath Sports Authority Field.

The Broncos advanced to Super Bowl 50 to play the Carolina Panthers at Levi's Stadium on Feb. 7. It took every last one of them to beat the Patriots 20-18 in front of 77,112 believers at Mile High.

See, we make this all about Manning. But that's all wrong. Maybe his signature moments, the ones he should be remembered for, unfolded off camera.

How he worked to come back from multiple neck surgeries and help the Broncos to two Super Bowls, and how he worked to return from a foot injury that cut his 18th season in half. There were no cameras in the operating room, or in the training facility where he threw pass after pass after pass with practice squad wide receiver Jordan Taylor and a handful of team managers.

"Throughout his entire injury process, every day he was coming in there to work hard," said Taylor, who caught more passes from Manning than any other player, despite never playing in a game. "He was even trying to get me better. There were some days he was correcting my route-running."

Now the Broncos are California Dreamin'. They are in the Super Bowl for the eighth time, seven of which included John Elway in a leading capacity. They were the best team in the AFC, a No. 1 seed that beat the No. 2 seed (twice), No. 3 seed, No. 4 seed (Houston, in the preseason), No. 5 seed and No. 6 seed. Their relentless defense seemed to crash down in waves against a pair of future Hall of Fame

Peyton Manning checks out the Lamar Hunt Trophy. Manning was 17 of 32 for 176 yards and threw two touchdown passes. (Mark Reis, The Gazette)

The Denver Broncos' 2015 Championship Season

quarterbacks, Brady and Ben Roethlisberger. They've won 11 games by a touchdown or less, in a manner only an adrenaline junkie could love.

"God is so good," Von Miller said, once he stopped dancing. "He gives you a second chance in life."

Gary Kubiak wasn't lying. It took all of them. It took Taylor, whom Manning nicknamed "Sunshine." It took offensive tackle Ryan Harris, who was unemployed and riding ATVs when the Broncos called him in June to help replace Ryan Clady.

"The Super Bowl? How am I even here?" Harris said. "I mean, are you serious?"

It took DeMarcus Ware. Asked to deliver the pregame speech Saturday night, Ware preached a doozy his teammates were still talking about the next day. First, Ware placed the 1998 Lombardi Trophy in the front of the room. Next, he said this: "The Patriots are coming into our house and trying to take what we built."

It even took Bill Belichick. Give ol' Hoodie a game ball. His odd decision to defer in overtime at the Jets prevented Denver from tripping to snowy, sinister Foxboro.

Goodness gracious did it take Vonnie Football. Miller gave the Patriots altitude sickness. He harassed Brady for 2.5 sacks and four quarterback hurries. His Wikipedia page in the third quarter was changed to "Tom Brady's Daddy."

"We have a motto on this team that iron sharpens iron and another man sharpens another man," Ware said.

It took all of the men. Manning is simply front and center because he's always been.

"To me, this victory is a great example of what this entire season has been like," said Manning, off to his fourth Super Bowl, first as supporting actor. "It hasn't been easy."

Manning was 17 of 32 for 176 yards. He threw two touchdown passes, double his total at Mile High before Sunday. After he improved to 3-1 against Belichick-Brady in AFC title games, Manning said, "It's not really time to reflect."

As it turns out, time can wait. ■

Wide receivers Emmanuel Sanders and Demaryius Thomas celebrate the Broncos' win by making angels in the confetti. (Mark Reis, The Gazette)

The Denver Broncos' 2015 Championship Season

General manager and Broncos Hall of Fame quarterback John Elway holds up the Lamar Hunt Trophy. (Christian Murdock, The Gazette)

Peyton Manning and Brock Osweiler celebrate Denver's 20-18 win in the AFC Championship. (Mark Reis, The Gazette)